CLASSIC
COUNTRY·PUBS

CLASSIC
COUNTRY·PUBS
A CAMRA GUIDE

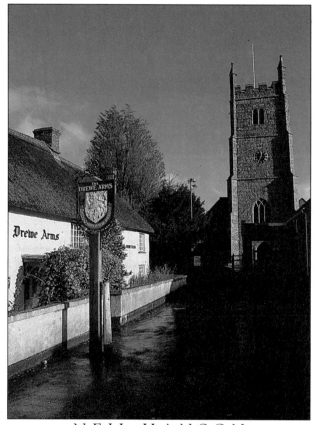

NEIL HANSON

PAVILION
MICHAEL JOSEPH

First published in Great Britain in 1987 by
Pavilion Books Limited
196 Shaftesbury Avenue, London WC2H 8JL
in association with Michael Joseph Limited
27 Wrights Lane, Kensington, London W8 5TZ

Designed by Andrew Barron Associates

Cartography by Reg Piggott

British Library Cataloguing in Publication Data

Hanson, Neil
   Classic country pubs.
   1. Hotels, taverns, etc.—Great Britain
   2. Great Britain—Description and travel—
   1971-   —Guide-books
   I. Title
   647′.944101   TX910.G7

ISBN 1-85145-114-5

Typeset by Dorchester Typesetting, Dorchester.
Printed and bound in Great Britain by
Hazell Watson & Viney Ltd, Aylesbury.

The photograph on page 3 is of the Drewe Arms, Drewsteignton, Devon

Picture Credits

Tom Ang/A & G Agency: 6, 8, 100, 101, 102, 104, 106, 107,
108, 110, 120, 121, 122, 123, 124, 125, 126, 129,
131, 132, 133, 135, 152, 153, 154; Batemans Brewery: 171, 173;
Britain on View (BTA/ETB): 11, 14, 15, 16, 17, 18, 19,
21, 26, 37, 77, 119, 155, 169, 178; Elgoods Brewery: 172;
Neil Hanson: 10, 22, 23, 25, 27, 32, 38, 39, 40, 41, 42, 43,
44 (above), 45, 47, 48, 51, 52, 53, 54, 79, 80, 81, 82, 83, 84, 85,
90, 93, 95, 96, 97, 98, 99, 103, 111, 113, 114, 115, 117,
118, 136, 137, 138, 139, 140, 141, 144, 146, 147, 148, 149, 150,
151, 157, 158, 159, 161, 162, 165, 166, 167, 190;
National Trust: 46; New Dimension Photography: 142, 143;
Linda Parry: 12, 13, 28, 29, 30, 35, 36, 44 (below), 49, 57, 59,
87, 88, 89, 175, 179, 180; Roger Protz: 164, 170, 174, 177, 184,
185, 186; Tim Webb: 168, 182, 183;
Jeremy Young/A & G Agency: title page, 55, 58, 61, 62, 63, 64,
65, 67, 68, 69, 70, 71, 72, 73, 74, 75, 76.

Contents

— 6 —
Preface
— 9 —
Acknowledgements
— 11 —
Introduction
— 21 —
To the Garden of England and the Downs
— 37 —
To Oxford and Shakespeare Country
— 55 —
To the West Country
— 77 —
To Wales and the Welsh Borders
— 99 —
To the Lake District
— 119 —
To the Scottish Borders
— 135 —
To the Yorkshire Moors and Dales
— 155 —
To the Peak District and the Midlands
— 169 —
To the Fens, the Broads and Constable Country
— 187 —
The Maps
— 191 —
Index of Pubs

Preface

Wall plaque in the Chequers, Ledsham, Yorkshire

There are about 70,000 pubs in Britain and to their regulars each one is probably a classic. To choose just one hundred out of them is a near impossible, though very enjoyable, task. There are a few pubs that would probably be on everybody's list; for the rest, scratch any pub-goer and you would get a different selection, but that is just what makes British pubs unique: they are as individual as the people who run them and the people who drink in them.

This individuality of our pubs, and the beers that they serve, is their greatest strength. Despite all the attempts of our giant brewers to impose standardisation, it is pleasant to note that local tastes, local characters, and quite a few local eccentrics, still survive and prosper.

I have set out to describe some country classics that everyone knows and a few that none but the initiates have ever heard of. My journey begins and ends in London, but you can start and finish where you like. Best of all, try some of these classics, but take the time to make your own pub discoveries too; round any corner, down any side-road, there just might be the best pub you have ever seen in your life. . . .

As well as the pubs themselves, I have tried to point out a few features of the landscape along the way and to tell something of the history of each area. This not only makes the journey more rewarding, it is also relevant to the nature of the pubs themselves; they did not grow up in isolation, they developed in response to the character and traditions of their communities.

Along the way I passed many excellent pubs that could easily have been included in this book; the problem was always too many, rather than too few classic pubs. One omission should be explained, however. You will not find any pubs from north of the Firth of

Forth in these pages. This is not because there are no good ones in Scotland, but because Scottish bars are distinctively different from English pubs. They merit a book on their own, which we hope to do soon. Meanwhile, I have contented myself with a selection from the Borders to the Firth of Forth.

There is no magic formula that makes one pub a classic and another just a boozer, the ingredients are as elusive as sunshine in an English summer. Some are classics for their architecture, some for their location, some because they are unique – the highest, the smallest, the oldest. Most, though, are classics for an indefinable mix of character and atmosphere: don't try too hard to analyse it, just sit back and enjoy it.

One thing all classic pubs have in common is the quality of the licensees. It doesn't matter how well-designed the pub, how fascinating its history, how breathtaking the views, how splendid the facilities; if the licensees are lazy or unfriendly, the pub will not even be a decent local, never mind a classic. If the licensees know their business, however, their pub will have a warm, friendly atmosphere. It will be a place where people of all ages can mix happily together, where regulars feel at home and where strangers are made welcome. Depending on your mood, you can join in the conversation at the bar, have a game of darts or dominoes, or find a quiet corner to read a paper or have a chat.

Good licensees also keep their beer in excellent condition. Some people may feel that the Campaign for Real Ale, which devotes itself to the preservation of traditional beer and traditional pubs to drink it in, attaches too much importance to a pub's beer. The truth is that if licensees are willing to take the time and trouble to look after the beer, the chances are that they will be equally willing to take the time and trouble to look after their customers too.

As well as being keepers of good ale, good licensees are founts of all wisdom, good listeners, wise counsellors, settlers of arguments, diplomats, comedians, philosophers, cooks, bottle-washers or all-in wrestlers, as the occasion demands: they are the upholders of one of our most valuable national institutions, our local pubs.

Forget our castles, cathedrals and stately homes – the British pub is everybody's heritage, an integral part of our social life for over a thousand years. Here are one hundred country classics, traditional British pubs, serving traditional British beer. Long may they continue!

The pub cat enjoying the warmth of the fire at the St Kew Inn, St Kew, Cornwall

Stained glass door in the Castle Inn, Lydford, Devon

Acknowledgements

Though my name appears in splendid isolation on the cover of this book, I owe a considerable debt of gratitude to many other people. Foremost among them are Roger Protz and Tim Webb, who have given me great help with research, photography and writing. The sections covering East Anglia, the West Country and Shakespeare Country, in particular, owe much to their labours and enthusiastic research!

Jill Adam kept an eye on the wood while I was working my way up through the trees, and she helped with many last-minute problems. My colleagues at CAMRA, Jo Bates, Sally Bennell, Carol Couch, Iain Dobson and Malcolm Harding, provided everything from assistance with the work to a sympathetic ear in the pub at the end of the long, hard days. Many CAMRA members and even a few chance acquaintances in pubs provided useful recommendations.

Colin Webb, Viv Bowler and Judith Wilson at Pavilion Books offered much valuable advice and criticism, and Andrew Barron took my slightly woolly concept for *Classic Country Pubs* and turned it into a classic piece of design. The photographers Tom Ang, Linda Parry and Jeremy Young struggled through a typical British summer and caught at least some of the fleeting rays of sunshine that penetrated the rain. Most of the colour photographs were shot using Fuji 50 and 1600 transparency film. I am also indebted to the British Tourist Board and the National Trust for the use of some of their material.

Lastly, a less specific, but no less substantial debt of gratitude. My knowledge of British pubs is the result of a personal voyage of discovery over many years, but my love of the countryside owes much to the wisdom and the example of my uncle, Torsten Bailey, who first opened my eyes to the beauty of the British landscape.

Opposite: Gleaming brass and a roaring fire sum up the appeal and the warm welcome of a fine traditional inn

Introduction

T he origins of the British pub are lost in the mists of alcohol, but it has been one of the pillars of British social life for centuries. It has evolved in a multitude of different forms, yet the coaching inn, the humble country local, the upmarket city hotel and the basic town boozer share enough of a common heritage for us to enter each one with reasonable confidence about what we shall find.

The pub has survived because, rather than being the creation of brewery architects, designers, landlords or customers, it has evolved down the centuries, adapting to changing circumstances without losing its essential character. Why the British pub should be so much more than just a watering-hole, when in most other countries a bar is a bar is a bar, remains a bit of a mystery; that the pub is a very special place is confirmed by the delight of every foreign visitor on discovering it for the first time.

At one time ale was purely a home-produced item and the first public houses were quite literally houses where, because of the skill of the home brewer, the public would

Above: A private bar in a public house; etched and engraved glass is a feature of many fine pub interiors
Opposite: Pure, natural ingredients for a pure, natural product; barley-malt at the Donnington Brewery near Stow-on-the-Wold

meet to drink the house ale and talk. These pubs or ale-houses became the focus of social life. Births, marriages and deaths would be celebrated or commemorated there, wages were often distributed there – and each man, whether he was a drinker or not, would have ale money deducted from his pay. The pub became wedded to the fabric of daily life so strongly that it has survived the turmoils of civil war, industrial revolution and the worst that the twentieth century can do to it.

In Roman Britain, the cities and towns each had their taverna, with a garland of vine or evergreen leaves hanging outside, the symbol of Bacchus, god of wine. The custom of having an illustrated sign outside the pub derives from this, most obviously a name such as the Hollybush. At a time of widespread illiteracy, illustrated signs were used by every trade and profession. The practice has fallen into disuse in every other trade, but inn signs remain. In the 1960s some large brewers tried to replace their individual pub signs with a corporate 'house style', but the adverse reaction of their customers persuaded them hastily to re-think their plans.

A name as ancient as the Bush is the Chequers, the emblem of those inn-keepers who also acted as money-lenders. Excavation at Pompeii unearthed examples of this sign. The Romans brought the chequer board with them to Britain, and it remained with us after their departure.

The development of inn signs mirrored changes in society as a whole. For example, the defeat of the House of York in the Wars of the Roses led to a wholesale change in pub signing. Richard III's death at Bosworth Field was a relatively easy matter for opportunist landlords – his crest, a white boar, was simply converted to the blue boar of the Earl of Oxford, a supporter of the winning side, the Tudors.

King's and Queen's Heads and Arms proliferated as landlords sought to link their pub with the reigning monarch, particularly after Henry VIII's dissolution of the monasteries, when countless Pope's Heads became King's Heads almost overnight! The same is true of the heraldic devices of powerful families – Lions and Horses of various colours, Eagles and Bears with and without Ragged Staffs, were frequently featured on inn signs.

The Church was a powerful early influence on signs, and the influence remained strong even after the Reformation – sometimes in code. The Goat and Compasses is a corruption of 'God encompass us', designed to keep the Puritans at bay, but names like the

Angel and the Salutation were clear evidence of 'popery', and disappeared under Cromwell's rule, to be replaced with more prosaic names like the Soldier. Saint George, the patron saint of England, lost his halo under Cromwell, hence the large number of pubs just called the George.

Pub names like the Mitre (the insignia of St Peter), the Lamb (Christ) and, surprisingly, the Hope and Anchor all have religious connections – hope being the anchor of the soul. Crusade fever led to a rash of Saracen's Heads and particularly to the sign of one of the many 'England's oldest inns', the Trip to Jerusalem in Nottingham, where crusaders on their way to the Holy Land paused for refreshment.

Other pub signs were a continuation of pre-Christian beliefs in defiance of the Church. The Green Man harks back to pagan rites, and also possibly to the wild men who covered themselves in greenery and attacked travellers – the legend of Robin Hood started with them.

As trades congregated in certain districts, so the inns where much of their business was transacted came to carry their insignia. The Fleece represents the wool trade, the Three Tuns the vintners, the Three Compasses and the Axe and Compasses the carpenters. Other common names include the Masons Arms, the Miners Arms, and so on.

There are also many far less obvious pub signs. The gruesome one for the Quiet Woman – a beheaded woman carrying her head under her arm – could at first, like one variant of the Nag's Head, be taken as a crude anti-feminist statement. In fact the Quiet Woman refers to a seventh-century saint who had her head cut off by her stepmother and brother for no particularly good reason. Legend has it that she picked up her head and carried it to the altar before dying.

The Black Boy does not refer to racial differences, but commemorates the incident when Charles I, after his defeat at the Battle of Worcester, dressed in woodman's clothes and darkened his face with soot to disguise himself. He was hidden in the branches of an oak tree while Cromwell's men searched the woods for him, which gave rise to another, very widespread sign – the Royal Oak.

The image we have of the cosy country inns of the past was not always true; for centuries the countryside was the province of lawless bands of robbers, and travel was the prerogative of merchants and pilgrims. Though the inns were primitive, usually with rush-strewn floors on which the guests would spend a communal night, they were recognised as places of relative safety. Richard II passed a law in 1393 compelling landlords to display a sign showing that they offered sanctuary as well as board and lodging, though many travellers preferred the protection of the local lord or of a monastic hospice.

True coaching inns did not really develop until after the first of the Turnpike Acts in 1663. Before then the roads were so appalling that travel by coach was virtually impossible – it was more customary to yoke up oxen than horses if a journey absolutely had to be undertaken – and travel by horse could only safely be undertaken in summer – safely

Inn sign from the Whynot Inn, Andover, Hampshire

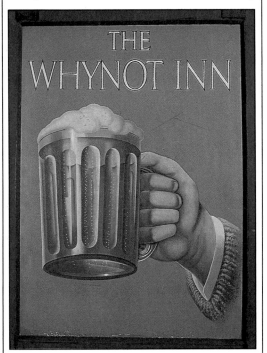

except for highwaymen, that is.

As transport improved, the changing face of travel was reflected in pub signs. The Pack Horse gave way to the Coach & Horses, which in turn yielded to the Narrowboat and then the Railway. Search hard enough and no doubt you'll find the Jet Engine and the Sputnik, too. New signs continue to appear, celebrating more or less plausible events or people – the Sober Journalist, the Modest TV Personality, the Truthful Politician. Others commemorate someone or something which will be forgotten before long, leaving future regulars to come up with explanations for the name which may well be every bit as preposterous as some of the ones I've given here! The Leg of Mutton, for example, is claimed to have originated because the artistry of one painter commissioned to produce a sign for the Star and Garter – a leg bearing the emblem of the royal court – was less than inspiring.

Another feature which makes the British pub outstanding is our obsession with games, as obvious in the pub as it is on the playing fields of Eton. The prerequisites of a good pub game are that it may be played and enjoyed by people of all levels of skill, that it should provide infinite variations around a simple theme, and that, while competitive, it should enhance rather than detract from the companionship, conversation and the taking of a modicum of drink for which everybody is there in the first place!

Darts is the most popular pub game – its

The symbol of the West Country Brewery – The 'Best in the West' – at Hay-on-Wye, Hereford & Worcester

slang name 'arrows' probably dates back to the time when longbowmen whittled down their feathered arrows to play an early form of the game. Though the standard board is becoming increasingly dominant, there are still many regional variants. There is a miniature Manchester board made of elm wood, a 'fives' board numbered in multiples of five used in some parts of the South East, a Yorkshire board with no trebles, and sundry other obscure variations.

Second only to darts in popularity is dominoes, a game often associated with gnarled old men in smoky taprooms, but in fact played by all sorts of people in all sorts of pubs. Such is the obsessive concentration displayed by some dedicated players, that World War III could break out without any disturbance to the measured clack of ivory laid on a table. I witnessed a game one New Year's Eve when the taproom door burst open

Clive Hollis at work in the Cooper's Shop at the Theakston Brewery, Masham, Yorkshire

and a man in a kilt, playing the bagpipes entered and circled the room, leading a motley crew of people dressed for a fancy dress party. It was, to say the least, an arresting sight, but the first sound to be heard as the piper and his entourage disappeared was a voice from the 'doms' table asking who had played the double four!

The third almost universal pub game is cribbage, or 'crib'. Like dominoes, one of its prime attractions is that it requires no physical effort, being played from a sedentary position. There are a few chess pubs, but the game is too intense, too cerebral to qualify as a true pub game (and too long for licensing hours). Draughts also has a few adherents, and Nine Men's Morris – a bizarre and ancient game – has staged something of a revival in recent years.

Shove Ha'penny is another archetypal pub game, played with polished coins which float like hovercraft across boards that have been polished until they shine like the Holy Grail. Any attempt to place a beer glass on the board is treated as a crime as serious as insulting Queen Guinevere or spitting in the aforementioned Grail – don't do it if you want to live to see closing-time! There is a local variant of the game, played in Dorset on a 'Swanage board' – a piece of mahogany of prodigious length, with the scoring area almost out of sight at the far end.

There are many variations on the theme of skittles. Table skittle games include Devil

among the Tailors, in which a ball suspended on a cord is swung into a group of skittles, and Northamptonshire Hood Skittles, in which circular, flat 'cheeses' are bounced off the padded sides of the skittle table. In Oxfordshire they play Aunt Sally, which requires six beechwood balls, but only one pin. You can also play several varieties of alley skittles, notably in the South West, where there are any number of variations, and in Nottinghamshire and Leicestershire, where they play the Long Alley version.

Quoits, once commonplace when the raw material – horseshoes – was rather more plentiful, has declined a great deal, though there are still thriving quoits leagues in East Anglia and Durham. In some games actual horseshoes are used, but more common are round metal rings that are thrown on to a 'hob' embedded in a clay pit. Indoor quoits is played in the West Midlands under the name of Dobbers, and in a small area of Suffolk where the game is called Flat Board. A similar sort of game, found in a scattering of pubs throughout Britain, is Ring the Bull, in which competitors try to toss a ring over a horn or a hook on the wall.

Pool tables are a common feature of many pubs; purists dismiss them, however, preferring the older (and more British) game of bar billiards, which is particularly useful in small spaces since you only play from one end of the table.

One game that has mushroomed in

Hop-growing strings near Headcorn, Kent. Hop-vines growing over a trellis of poles and strings are a traditional feature of the Kent landscape

British pubs during recent years has been the trivia quiz, in which teams compete to see who has the greatest store of absolutely useless information. Since the source of most good pub conversations is useless information, this development can only strengthen the social role of the pub in the future!

There are several more or less plausible outdoor games associated with pubs. Some are genuinely ancient, some even date back to pre-Christian rituals; others are as genuinely ancient as a Julius Caesar one pound note, but none the less entertaining for that. Bat and Trap, played in Kent, and Knur and Spell from east and west of the Pennines, are the likely ancestors of the quintessentially British games of cricket and golf. Unlike cricket they don't involve playing for several days with only a fair chance of a result; but they do involve hitting a small projectile with a piece of wood.

There are also numerous drinking games, but without exception these are designed to render all the participants drunk and incapable in the shortest possible time and so don't fit too happily into any book about good pubs. Pubs are places to enjoy oneself in company with others, not at the expense of others. Drunks, bores and troublemakers are the bane of pubs, and good landlords discourage or terminate their excesses. If they don't, they find their other customers have voted with their feet and moved to the pub down the road.

The large number of electronic games that come and go with the passing years are not true pub games, in the sense that they usually require one person to play in isolation rather than a group of people in friendly company. Most rely on novelty for their appeal, and adherents usually get bored quickly and move on to some newer storehouse of electronic delights.

It isn't necessary to play pub games to enjoy pubs; it isn't even necessary to drink beer; but if you don't, you're depriving yourself of the chance of discovering liquid gold. You'll be fortunate if you don't encounter at least one pint of vinegar along the way – but that merely serves to highlight the excellence of a really fine ale.

Traditional British beer – 'real ale', in CAMRA-speak – is beer that is brewed only from natural ingredients: malted barley, hops, yeast and pure water. It is neither pasteurised nor sterilised, so it continues to condition in the cask, maturing and improving in flavour until it is served, dispensed either by gravity straight from the barrel or pulled through a

The Darley Brewery's 'Symbol of Good Ale' at Carlton, Yorkshire

handpump. The beer will be served in accordance with the conventions of the area you are in – either flat or with a 'collar' or 'head' – and wherever you are in the country, you will find that there are countless regional variations on the theme of beer – paler, darker, hoppier, maltier, weaker, stronger.

The alternative is keg beer, which has been conditioned at the brewery and which may contain all sorts of adjuncts and additives as well as the malt and hops – everything from potatoes and onions to arsenic and formaldehyde have been added to beer. The resulting mixture is heavily chilled and dispensed under carbon dioxide pressure to conceal its

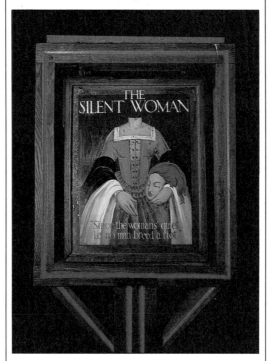

The gruesome sign for the Silent Woman, Wareham, Dorset commemorates a seventh-century saint

relative lack of flavour. It bears the same relation to real ale as factory cheese does to properly matured farmhouse cheese.

Though our national drink comes in a bewildering number of different brews, there are four basic beer 'styles': mild, bitter, strong ale and stout. If you sample the range at all the hundred country classics in this book you will have tried a fair cross-section, but there are some that no self-respecting student of the brewer's art should miss.

Mild ales were once vastly popular but are now in decline, even in their midland and north-western heartlands. 'Mild' refers to the flavour; they are usually less well-hopped than bitters, and they are usually weaker in alcoholic strength, too. Try Banks's pale mild, Ansells darker brew, or the richer, darker Thwaites or Highgate milds.

Bitter is *the* British beer, with countless

superb regional variations to be investigated. Adnam, Bateman, Batham, Brain, Brakspear, Donnington, Fuller, Gale, Holt, Hook Norton, Robinson, Shepherd Neame, Taylor, Tetley, Young – the roll of honour could go on for ever but you'll want to discover a few for yourself.

A little further up the strength table are the 'best' bitters. These are too strong for all-night sessions unless you've been in strict training for some time, but they include two beers that would be on most drinkers' lists of the best beers in Britain – Marston Pedigree and Timothy Taylor Landlord.

Even stronger, and more dangerous to the inexperienced, are the extra strong ales! The pale, hoppy Fuller ESB and the rich, dark Theakston Old Peculier (with its peculiar spelling) are both superb examples of the style, but unless you're very confident I'd start with a half pint. . . . Most small breweries produce their own extra strong beer, often with an appropriately cautionary name like Dogbolter, Headbanger or Moonraker – two pints and you're in orbit!

Stout is the last great beer style, and 'the black stuff' – Guinness – is what most people immediately think of. It's undoubtedly one of the world's great beers, but needs to be supped in the Republic of Ireland to be enjoyed at its best. If you can't make the journey, try Strathalbyn Beardmore Stout. I think it's better than Guinness, but that isn't an opinion to be expressed too loudly in Dublin!

Whatever you're drinking, you may if you're lucky come across one of the greatest of all traditions associated with British pubs – 'lates'. Licensing laws in England and Wales are still regulated by a system that was introduced by the teetotal Lloyd George during the First World War to stop munitions workers from drinking too much. For seventy years it has been impossible to drink in an English pub in the afternoon or late at night without breaking the law. While Scotland and Ireland have sensibly liberal drinking laws, in England and Wales we still await salvation; but in the meantime, in every town and in an awful lot of villages too, the dedicated pursuit of making a fool of the law goes on.

We all dream of the day when we can finish drinking at our leisure rather than cramming the last beer in just because the pub is about to close. In the meantime, however, beating the licensing system is perhaps the most enjoyable pub game there is. Good hunting!

Neil Hanson

To the Garden of England and the Downs

'Up the village, that is higher up the hill, there are the old cottages round the church, the street itself, and then a large school, all of this before the main village green charms with trees, pubs, motionless windmill and even stiller cricketers.'

THE RIVERS AND THE DOWNS
MICHAEL BALDWIN

— 22 —

The English countryside delights its foreign visitors with a series of land-scapes in miniature. To come from, say, the grain prairies of North America to a country where almost every turn in the road opens up a new vista can be a delight. If this is true of England as a whole, it is particularly so of its south-eastern corner, known as the Garden of England. There are no mountains or moorlands to be found here, but it contains almost every other kind of English landscape in an area that can be spanned comfortably in a day.

It is also an area steeped in antiquity and rich in historical and literary associations.

In summer, the Carpenters Arms, Eastling, is almost smothered in flowers Opposite: Familiar features of old Kent buildings; a massive brick chimney and weather-boarded walls. The Carpenters Arms, Eastling

Caesar's Roman legions landed here in 55 BC, and the Norman conquerors, the last success-ful invaders of British soil, defeated the English at the Battle of Hastings in 1066. Chaucer's pilgrims crossed this landscape on their way to Canterbury, and the ancient walls of its castles, towns and villages could tell tales of Richard the Lionheart, Elizabeth I and other, less noble denizens of English history, such as the infamous Hawkhurst smuggling gang.

The reason for the name the Garden of England becomes obvious as soon as you leave the suburban sprawl of London behind you. Take the M2 east to Faversham and you are quickly into the rolling landscape of the North Downs. This is country without hard, cutting edges; everything is soft, lush and rounded; it is a country of gentle hills, with fertile soil and a soft climate.

Kent grows much of England's fruit, it also grows ninety per cent of our hops, the ingredient that gives our beer its aroma and its bitter taste. Armies of itinerant labourers and holidaying Londoners used to descend on Kent for the fruit- and hop-picking. Now much of the work is done by machinery, and the hop-growing industry in particular is hard pressed, but the Kentish landscape is still dominated by the forests of hop-poles over which the hop-plants grow, and the tall conical roofed oast-houses in which they are dried.

Faversham is home to Shepherd Neame, one of the Kentish brewers who support their local industry by brewing hop-filled beer which has an aroma and a bitter flavour that can take your breath away. To sample their brew at our first country classic pub, turn off the M2 towards Faversham, turn left on to the A2, then left again at the end of the school playing fields on to Brogdale Road. Follow it as it winds past oast-houses, hedgerows and orchards until you reach Eastling.

The village church at Eastling is mentioned in 'Domesday Book', and the Carpenters Arms dates from 1380. Under the steep pitched roof is a games room with an inglenook, church pew seats and bar billiards as well as the ubiquitous darts, and there is another ingle-nook in the small bar with an old bread oven set into it. The floors and walls are old brick, and the oak beams are decorated with garlands of hops. You can eat in the bar, or there is a small board-walled supper room where you can enjoy the *à la carte* menu, centred around game such as casserole of pheasant, jugged hare, partridge and wild duck in winter and fish, including the excellent Admiral's Pie full of scallops, prawns and oysters in summer.

At one time Eastling was the centre of the Kent cherry orchards, and cherry auctions were held outside the weatherboard and brick pub. Sit on the benches on the lawn and, depending on the season, enjoy the pretty gardens, the smell of blossom on the breeze, the scent of roses and jasmine growing on the outbuildings, the hollyhocks all around the pub and the cotoneaster and creeper covering the walls.

Eastling is just four miles from the Pilgrims Way, the route by which pilgrims such as those described in Chaucer's *Canterbury Tales* made their way to Canterbury, site of the murder of Thomas à Becket. Follow the A2 east to the city, past the fruit orchards and the lines of poplars standing sentinel over forests of hop-poles.

When you have looked at the ancient city and its cathedral, pick up the A2 south of the city and take the Bridge turning. Go straight over at the crossroads and follow the signs down a winding country lane past an

The Carpenters Arms
Licensee: Maureen Wright
Eastling, Kent
☎ Eastling (079 589) 234
11-3; 6-11

Shepherd Neame Master Brew Mild, Bitter, Stock Ale

Lunchtime & evening food. Accommodation. Garden. Families welcome.

ancient black weatherboarded and thatched barn to Pett Bottom, where you will find another delightful pub, the Duck Inn.

The Duck sits in a beautiful, tranquil setting, looking out over rolling countryside. It was built in 1623 and was originally a farm, part of a large estate. In 1849 it became an ale-house, doubling as a grocer's shop and it was only granted a full licence in 1904, when it was known as the Woodmans Arms. Its name was changed to the Duck in the 1960s.

The duck motif extends throughout the pub, carried on in duck tureens, decoy ducks, china ducks and even flying ducks. There is a small bar with an open fire and a boarded

The Duck Inn, Pett Bottom – hard to find, but well worth the effort

ceiling, a main bar with another fire, and a light and airy restaurant. The pub serves a very good Aberdeen Angus roast beef Sunday lunch and the restaurant menu changes every month.

There is a very wide choice of ales straight from the barrel, and you can enjoy your drinks outside if you wish, either in a lovely garden, at tables in the shade of a massive tree, or on the benches at the front of the inn, where Ian Fleming, creator of James Bond, once enjoyed his very dry martini, shaken but not stirred.

From the Duck, carry on the way you were travelling, turn right at the crossroads towards Hardres and Bossingham, left at the main road, right in Bossingham and left on to Stone Street, a Roman road running straight as an arrow to the south. If you miss your way, you will probably enjoy wandering through

The Duck Inn
Licensees: Les & Carol Boothright
Pett Bottom, Bridge, nr Canterbury, Kent
☎ Canterbury (0227) 830354
11.30-2.30; 6-10.30 (11 Friday, Saturday & summer). Closed Monday.

Fuller London Pride; Marston Pedigree; Shepherd Neame Master Brew Bitter; Wem Special Bitter

Lunchtime & evening food. Garden. Families welcome.

the byways of Kent and will get your bearings soon enough when you eventually emerge on to a main road.

Stone Street follows the line of a ridge, giving superb views down over the Weald of Kent to the west and towards the sea to the east. As it begins to descend, it becomes for a short while a 'hollow way', a sure sign of an ancient track. The effects of erosion on trackways stripped of vegetation by the feet of travellers and their animals gradually sink the track below the level of the surrounding country. Old hollow ways are like green, cool tunnels, burrowing between high earth banks, with a canopy of trees overhead.

A bedroom as old and traditional as the inn itself; the Mermaid Inn, Rye
Opposite: The cobbled street outside the Mermaid Inn leads down to the once-thriving harbour, where naval ships and those of smugglers both contributed to Rye's prosperity

As the street drops further, you come off the highlands of Kent into the flatlands of the Romney Marshes. Turn west at Lympne Castle, one of the many in this area, guarding the traditional invasion route into England. At Hamstreet, turn south across the Royal Military Canal and make for the beautiful town of Rye, perched on a hill above the marshlands.

E. V. Lucas said of Rye: 'We have seen many ancient towns in our progress through the County . . . but all have modern blood in their veins, Winchelsea and Rye seem almost wholly of the past', and little seems to have changed since then. There is little left of the town wall authorised by Richard the Lionheart as 'the greatest safeguard which could be made in these parts for the security of our kingdom', but it still seems to bind the town together.

Rye was one of the group of seaports, the Cinque Ports, so called because there were originally five: Hastings, Dover, Sandwich, Romney and Hythe. Later expanded to include Rye and Winchelsea, they provided the chief part of the navy and had many privileges in return. Rye was for a long period the chief English seaport, and thrived as much on

The Mermaid
Licensee: M. K. Gregory
Mermaid Street, Rye, East Sussex
☎ Rye (0797) 223065
11-2.30; 6-11

Fremlins Bitter; Wethered Bitter

Lunchtime & evening food. Accommodation. Garden.

smuggling as it did on legitimate naval activities.

The town is dominated by the fine church of St Mary the Virgin and the Ypres Tower, originally known as Baddings Tower, and built around 1250 as a defence against the French. Nearby is Lamb House, where the novelist Henry James lived for many years, and across the street is the old Customs House, an ironic location, for just around the corner, at the head of the steep, cobbled Mermaid Street, is the Mermaid Inn, for many years the haunt of smugglers including the notorious Hawkhurst gang.

Despite the archway in the centre of the inn, the Mermaid was never a coaching inn, for it is far older than the coaching age. The present half-timbered and creeper-covered inn dates from 1420, itself a rebuilding of an earlier inn that stood on the site, and further rebuilding occurred in the sixteenth century.

There are many English inns of similar age which have been ruined by the careless attentions and 'improvements' of their owners; the Mermaid is completely authentic and absolutely beautiful, drawing thousands of visitors from all over the world every year. There are massive oak beams, superb oak panelling, vast ingle-nook fireplaces, including one which is probably the largest in England, and a host of interesting features. Look up the chimney and you will see the 'priest hole', a hiding-place dating from the days when the Roman Catholic religion was suppressed and its adherents persecuted. There are secret passageways and stairs and fine panelled bedrooms in which you can spend the night in a four-poster bed.

The Mermaid is very much a hotel and restaurant as well as a pub. The food is good, with local specialities such as Romney Marsh lamb, and the bedrooms are comfortable as well as authentically old, which is not always the case in old buildings. If you can stay a few days, this is an excellent place from which to explore one of the most historic areas of England.

Just a few miles to the west of Rye is the site of the Battle of Hastings, the village of Battle, with its Abbey built by a grateful William the Conqueror. From there, travel north to the next classic pub, one with more recent historical connections, the Three Chimneys, one and a half miles west of Biddenden on the Sissinghurst road.

The Three Chimneys looks pleasant but nothing exceptional from the outside, but step inside and you begin to realise what an

The Three Chimneys, near Biddenden: an unusually-named pub with an unusual history

excellent pub you've come across. The furnishings are traditional, but, unlike many similar pubs, there is no feeling of being in an antique shop – the atmosphere is warm, welcoming and traditional – a proper country pub in the Home Counties – whatever next!

A series of interconnecting small rooms radiate off the central bar and the beer is served straight from the casks stillaged at the back. There are blazing open fires in cold weather and candles provide some of the lighting. A no-nonsense public bar has a good range of games and there's also a family room at the back where you can book a table and look out on to the lovely garden.

The food is imaginative and very good, the range of beers available is often bewildering, as is the name of the pub. The Three Chimneys is actually a corruption of *Les Trois Chemins*. French prisoners taken in the Seven Years War were kept at the nearby Sissinghurst Castle. They were allowed out 'en promenade' but were forbidden to go beyond the junction of the three lanes (*trois chemins*) at which the pub stands – hence the name.

From Biddenden, make your way south-west through Heathfield, making a small detour, if you like, to see the Sugar Loaf at Dallington, not one of our greatest monuments, but one of the most bizarre. The Sugar Loaf is a conical stone spire built in the original Brightling Park by 'Mad' Jack Fuller, an eighteenth-century squire and Member of Parliament. It is claimed that he

The Three Chimneys
Licensees: Christopher & Pippa Sayers
Nr Biddenden, Kent
☎ Biddenden (0580) 291472
11-2.30; 6-10.30
(11 Friday & Saturday)

Adnams Bitter; Fremlins Bitter; Goacher's Maidstone Ale; Godson Black Horse; Harvey BB; Marston Pedigree

Lunchtime & evening food until 10, Sunday lunch until 1.30. Garden. Families welcome in Garden Room (ring for reservations).

had it built as a replica of Dallington church spire, in order to win a bet he had made with a friend that the spire could be seen from his house in Brightling Park. From the Sugar Loaf, which is hollow and once housed a hermit, you can look across to Brightling Park House and another of Mad Jack's follies, a fake Roman temple.

A couple of miles west of Heathfield, turn off towards the village of Blackboys, then turn left on to the B2192 and you will come to the Blackboys Inn on the right-hand side. The inn, a black weatherboarded building dating from the fourteenth century, looks out on to a lawn shaded by horse-chestnut trees and a duckpond surrounded by yellow irises. The ducks are not the only livestock associated with the inn: the licensees also keep ponies, goats, hens, peacocks and two pigs at the back of the pub, where there is also a children's play area.

The Blackboys was built in 1389 from the timbers of a Portuguese trading ship, wrecked on the Sussex coast. Inside there is a rambling dark-panelled warren of rooms. Good bar food ranges from steaks to *moules catalanes*, and there is a restaurant menu with a fine selection of sea-food and specialities such as Guardsmen of Lamb, a thick cut through the rack of lamb, roasted and served with rosemary and wine gravy.

Many pubs in the South have been virtually turned into licensed restaurants; despite the quality of the food at the Blackboys, Patrick Russell was determined that it should retain a proper pub atmosphere. In that he has been completely successful, nowhere more so than in the solidly traditional public bar, with its ingle-nook fireplace and wooden tables.

The origin of the Blackboys name is the subject of at least three theories. Pubs called the Black Boy are usually named after Charles I. As well as his black-faced escape from the Battle of Worcester, his dark complexion earned him the contemptuous nickname 'the black boy' from the Levellers, who were a faction advocating total social and religious equality. Blackboys, however, far pre-dates Charles I.

Blackboys was a centre of the English iron industry from the thirteenth century. Sussex was known as the wooded county, and the three essentials of iron-making, wood, water and ironstone, were all readily available. One theory of the origin of the name is that the village and pub were named after the charcoal burners in the area; another that it was the test-firers, who tested the cannons

The Blackboys Inn
Licensee: Patrick Russell
Lewes Road, Blackboys,
East Sussex
☎ Framfield (082 582) 283
10-2.30; 6-10.30
(11 Friday, Saturday & summer)

Harveys XX, BB, XXX

Lunchtime & evening food. Garden. Families welcome.

Opposite: The ancient Blackboys Inn is an ideal pub for families on a sunny, summer afternoon. It has enough domestic animals to stock a small zoo

made there, who were the black-faced boys. The present landlord prefers the more poetic theory that his pub is named Blackboys from a corruption of the Old French 'blancs bois', meaning, perversely, the white woods, so called because of the preponderance of silver birches in the local woodlands.

Whatever the origins, be sure not to miss the Blackboys. It is a fine building, an excellent pub and a great place to take the children. They can play in the barn or among the trees in the orchard, there are animals to look at and even a set of stocks. There is so much for them to do outside that it is one pub where the presence of other people's children is not an intrusion into the blessed peace of those who have come to the pub to get away from their own!

To reach the next country classic, there is a long cross-country drive, following the A272 across Sussex and far into Hampshire. You may be tempted to miss it out, but if you do, you will be missing a pub that is one of the truly great pubs, the White Horse at Priors Green, also known as 'the Pub With No Name'.

As you travel west, the neatly ordered fields of Kent and Sussex begin to give way to the more open, rolling country of Hampshire, with its arable fields and tree-studded parkland. You pass through the lovely village of Petworth, with its scores of antique shops huddled in the shelter of Petworth House. You may well wish to see the House, with its magnificent parkland and its herds of deer.

The White Horse has no pub sign and is extremely hard to find, but it is the epitome of a fine, traditional British pub

Further west you will pass Cowdray Park, where the Prince of Wales shows off his skills on the polo field.

The South Downs rise around you as you travel up the valley of the Rother towards Petersfield. Keep travelling west through Petersfield but then turn north at the round-about immediately after the level crossing. Climb up the hill towards Steep, through the beautiful beechwoods, and keep straight on across the top of the downs until you reach a crossroads with the skeleton of a pub sign and a sign indicating East Tisted to the right. Take that turn and then take the second gravel track on your right.

You will arrive at a white-painted, flower-covered building in the middle of a field; only the rough wooden seats and tables under the trees, looking out over the superb views of the downs, suggest that the building may be a pub.

The White Horse was built in 1620 and served an old road, and, no doubt, a few smugglers, crossing the downs. The road was straightened out to take a more direct route long ago, leaving the White Horse stranded in the middle of a field. The pub itself probably never had a sign, and when the one at the crossroads disappeared it was never replaced, yet despite, or possibly because of this, 'the Pub With No Name' is constantly rediscovered by visitors. It has a better trade than many town centre pubs, and deservedly so; once you have found it, you will not forget it.

Step through the door and you are in one of the most atmospheric pub interiors you will ever see. There are two bars, each with big open fires, beams, antique settles and chairs, the gleam of polished brass, the dull shine of pewter. In one is a beautifully carved long-case clock. For a long time, part of the inn was a smithy, and what is now the bar was the kitchen, with a third big open fireplace.

The poet Edward Thomas, killed in the First World War, wrote his first published poem about the pub, and there is a wood carving on the wall to commemorate him. No juke box, canned muzak or electronic games can disturb the peaceful atmosphere which inspired him. Children are welcome to sit in the garden, but lack of space as well as the law prevents them from being allowed in the bar. Food is limited to snacks such as sandwiches, which are of excellent quality; in winter there is an old-fashioned, tasty and very filling country soup as well. You can buy country wines and sample a wide range of unusual and excellent ales, including 'No Name Bitter'.

The White Horse (The Pub With No Name)
Licensee: Jack Eddlestone
Priors Dean, nr Petersfield, Hampshire
☎ Tisted (042 058) 387
11-2.30; 6-10.30
(11 Friday, Saturday & summer)

Ballards Best Bitter; Draught Bass; Eldridge Pope Royal Oak; Gales HSB; Gibbs Mew Bishops Tipple; Marston Merrie Monk, Pedigree; Palmer Bitter; Ringwood 49er, No Name Bitter (Old Thumper); Wadworth 6X

Lunchtime & evening food (sandwiches & snacks only). Garden.

The White Horse has not been tarted up, turned into a restaurant, a hotel or a 'fun pub'; it remains a perfect example of a traditional British pub. It is ironic that our 'heritage' of Greek marbles, Dutch paintings and French furniture, and the stately homes that are the province of a tiny proportion of us, are 'saved for the nation' at tremendous cost. Meanwhile, our true heritage, the vernacular buildings, the churches and pubs which are common to the experience of the vast majority of us, are sold, altered and even demolished with scarcely a word of protest. Be grateful for wonderful pubs like the White Horse, and enjoy them while you can. Lose them and, as Hilaire Belloc said, 'Drown your empty selves, for you have lost the last of England.'

If you have now travelled far enough afield for one day, turn back and retrace your route through Petworth as far as Pulborough, then turn to the north on the A29, the old Roman Stane Street, and follow it until just before you reach Ockley, where you will find a lane on the left that takes you to Oakwoodhill. The name of the village varies between that, Oakwood Hill and Okewoodhill, depending on which sign you are looking at, but all are undeniably the same place, so there is no danger of getting lost in the oak woods which give the village its name.

The Punch Bowl in Oakwood Hill is a pretty, tile-hung building under a steep, moss-encrusted roof. The bar has a massive brick ingle-nook, oak beams and huge flagstones set with solid, scrubbed pine tables. There is a little dining room down a step and through an arch and upstairs is a large room which doubles as a children's room in the daytime. The Oak Bar is a no-nonsense public bar with more scrubbed pine tables, an old oak settle and a dartboard.

You can sit outside on wooden benches in front of the pub, and there are several terraced areas with honeysuckle growing around them, where you can enjoy the peace and quiet of the countryside, looking out across the village cricket field, just over the road, to the oak woods beyond.

Leaving Oakwood Hill, rejoin the road north which passes through the lovely village of Ockley. The emblem of the village, an oak tree, is fixed to the Ockley sign, and as well as its oak trees, there is a huge village green surrounded by a series of pretty old brick and half-timbered houses, and there are ducks and geese on the pond.

The Punch Bowl
Licensees: Robert & Shirley Chambers
Oakwood Hill, nr Ockley, Surrey
☎ Oakwood Hill (030 679) 249
10.30-2.30; 5.30-10.30 (11 Friday, Saturday & summer)

Hall & Woodhouse Badger Best Bitter, Tanglefoot; King & Barnes Sussex Bitter, Draught Festive; Young Special Bitter

Lunchtime & evening food. Families welcome. Barbecues in summer.

The Punch Bowl, near Ockley, is a timeless and peaceful country inn, surrounded by oak woods

Villages like Ockley, lovely though they are, do have a strange fossilised character to them. Villages tend to develop organically, but once they have become the exclusive preserve of wealthy commuters, they cease to develop at all, remaining unaltered, lovingly tended and perfectly preserved; forever amber if not forever Ambridge.

It is not difficult to forget how much fine country there still is within easy reach of London; we must be eternally grateful to the Green Belt, which has contained the outward spread of London's suburbs. The landscape north of Ockley on the way to Dorking is as rich and private as the people who live in it. The rolling country is studded with hedges, trees and woods that conceal the houses set in it from a casual glance. This is commuter territory, emptying every morning as the human wave pours north to London, filling again in the evening as the ebb brings them back.

Just before you reach Dorking, take the A25 east. On the outskirts of Reigate, the road turns and twists through some scrubby woodland, and when you emerge the village green of Reigate Heath is on your right. Take the turning which leads down past the houses facing the green and turn left after a few hundred yards into Bonny's Road, an unmade road which crosses the golf course. Bear right as soon as you have crossed the course and you will see the Skimmington Castle before you at the top of the rise.

The Skimmington Castle is a very old

Skimmington Castle
Licensee: Andrew Fisher
Reigate Heath, Surrey
☎ Reigate (073 72) 43100
10.30-2.30; 5.30-10.30
(11 Friday, Saturday & summer)

Friary Meux Bitter; Ind Coope Burton Ale; Tetley Bitter

Lunchtime & evening food. Garden. Families welcome.

pub, but there is an extension built on to the front which disguises the great age of the original building. The wood-panelled bar has a collection of smokers' pipes hanging from the ceiing, there are pewter tankards and even a stuffed badger and a stuffed fox among the bric-à-brac behind the bar. You can enjoy your drinks looking down the lane to the golf course from the windows of the front bar, or from the benches outside; there are also some rough wooden benches in a small, tree-shaded garden behind the pub.

You can also sit in the older part of the building at the back, in the small dark-panelled bar or in the parlour where there is a

The Skimmington Castle, Reigate Heath, a fine 'nineteenth hole' for the nearby golf course

huge ingle-nook, with a bread oven set into one side of it. Down a narrow flight of steps is a tiny room where children can be left to destroy space invaders while you order a drink at the bar. The bar food includes several 'Bill Barnes' Specials (obviously a man with a large appetite), and you can even order chipped potatoes with or without their skins.

Over the door leading through to the back of the pub is a quotation from Samuel Johnson which still sums up much of the appeal of a good pub, some two hundred years after it was written. 'There is no private house in which people can enjoy themselves as at a capital tavern. You are sure you are welcome and the more good things you call for, the welcomer you are. There is nothing which has yet been contrived by man by which so much happiness is produced as by a good tavern or inn.'

To Oxford and Shakespeare Country

'All around, from every quarter, the stiff, clayey
soil of the arable fields crept up; bare, brown and
windswept for eight months out of the twelve.
Spring brought a flush of green wheat and there
were violets under the hedges and pussy-willows
out beside the brook . . . but only for a few weeks
in later summer had the landscape real beauty.'

LARK RISE TO CANDLEFORD
FLORA THOMPSON

London to Oxford and then on to Stratford-upon-Avon is one of the most well-worn tourist routes in England. One way to make the journey is to hammer up the M40 in a fast car to Oxford. After a pause to see the sights and allow the blood pressure to subside and the adrenalin gland to stop pumping, you can join the caravan and coach convoy on the A34, grinding ever westwards to Shakespeare country.

If you are more interested in seeing some of England's most beautiful countryside, towns and villages than the back of the vehicle in front, however, avoid the motorways like the plague. Travel out to the

The Crooked Billet at Stoke Row, once Nobby Harris' kingdom, but now ruled by a new landlord

beautiful Thameside town of Henley, have a pint or two of Brakspear's excellent beer in one of the many characterful pubs and then lose yourself in the heart of England for an hour or two.

Set off, refreshed, for Oxford and turn off the main road anywhere. You'll travel down narrow, winding country lanes where the sunlight filters through a canopy of leaves and you can stop the car and wander among the trees for an hour or so. You will find lovely villages tucked away in the beech woods of the Chilterns, and in almost every one, you will find a superb traditional pub.

If you are lucky, you will come across Stoke Row; if you are luckier still, you'll find the narrow winding lane that leads down to the Crooked Billet – the pub that time forgot. Turn left off the A423 five miles west of Henley, follow the Stoke Row sign.

The Crooked Billet
Licensee: Ben Salter
Newlands Lane/Nottwood Lane, Stoke Row, Oxfordshire
☎ Checkendon (0491) 681048
10.30-2.30; 6-11

Brakspear Mild, Pale Ale, Special Bitter, Old

Lunchtime & evening food. Families welcome. Garden.

Turn down the lane east of, and on the same side of the road as the Cherry Tree (also well worth a visit) and you will come to the Crooked Billet.

It stands as a reminder of the way rural pubs used to be a hundred and more years ago. Geese and bantams peck in the yard and a path winds into the beech woods from which generations of landlords brought timber to be turned for chair legs in the barn alongside the inn. It was in the same family for over a hundred years and owes much of its unspoilt charm to the character of Nobby Harris, the last of the family line, now sadly retired from the inn.

The Royal Standard of England, Forty Green. The name was granted to the inn by a grateful Charles I, who hid in its roof timbers after the Battle of Worcester

There is no bar in the Crooked Billet; the beer is drawn straight from the cask in the cellar and carried through to the customers. Have a pint with the new landlord, Ben Salter, also a Brakspear's landlord for many years, in rooms dominated by vast stone fireplaces and drink a toast to a bit of Old England that deserves to last for ever.

Before you move on, take a few minutes to look round Stoke Row – a typically English village containing an incongruously Indian-style 'Maharajah's Well' – a nineteenth-century gift to drought-stricken Stoke Row from the Maharajah of Benares, who had befriended an Englishman from the area.

If, despite my blandishments, you find yourself on the M40, instead of in the heart of the Chiltern beech woods, you are still not beyond salvation. Leave it at junction 2 and within five miles you could

The Royal Standard of England
Licensees: Philip Eldridge & Alan Wainwright
Forty Green, Buckinghamshire
☎ Beaconsfield (049 46) 3382
10.30-2.30; 5.30-11

Eldridge Pope Royal Oak; Marston Pedigree, Owd Rodger; Samuel Smith OBB

Lunchtime & evening food. Garden. Family room.

A stone tortoise embedded in the wall of the Royal Standard of England

find yourself in one of the most famous, historic and jam-packed inns in England. Take the A40 to Beaconsfield, then the B474 and follow the signs to Forty Green off to the right. The Royal Standard of England is one of the many claimants to the title of England's oldest inn.

It is certainly around nine hundred years old and is filled to the rafters with antique powder flasks, warming pans, bugles, swords, muskets, pewter tankards, ship's settles and blackened oak beams. The beams have played host to at least one distinguished visitor – Charles I – who hid amongst them above the room that now bears his name, during his flight from the Battle of Worcester in 1651. On his restoration in 1660, Charles granted the inn its present unique title.

The rambling collection of dark, candle-lit rooms is best seen in the glow of a fire from one of the great fireplaces in winter. In summer you can sit on the terrace outside or fight your way through the crowds to one of the best-looking, and best-tasting, cold buffets you could wish to meet. The pub has its own bread and pies, excellent cheeses and a chutney which is claimed to descend from a recipe 300 years old. Food prices are everything you would expect in an historic and very popular pub in stockbroker country.

If you want to know how busy the Royal Standard gets on Sunday lunchtimes, just note the size of the car-park (one of the largest in the western hemisphere), but don't be deterred from visiting it. A pub with such history and character could easily have been turned into the most twee and ghastly kind of tourist trap. It has not – it is a classic, and well worth missing a couple of motorway service stations for.

Now that you are off the motorway, let me lead you to a different, but equally excellent pub – the Lions of Bledlow. Travelling north on the B4009 towards Princes Risborough, turn right one mile beyond Chinnor. The turn is unsigned, but if you miss it you can take the Bledlow Ridge turn (the next on the right) and turn right again into the village.

The Lions of Bledlow can be packed with tourists; it's just as likely to be packed with locals, and after a walk through the beech woods and over the Chiltern hills on a frosty winter morning, it's a delight to settle down for a well-earned drink, warmed by the fire blazing in its brick ingle-nook fireplace. In warmer weather, you can take your drinks out to a terrace or lawns at the back or, better

The Lions of Bledlow
Licensee: F. J. McKeown
Bledlow, Buckinghamshire
☎ Princes Risborough (084 44) 3345

Courage Directors; Wadworth 6X; Young Bitter; Bulmers Cider; Guest Beers

Lunchtime & evening food (except Sunday evening). Restaurant. Family room.

The village green outside the Lions of Bledlow. What better place to spend a sunny, summer afternoon?

still, on to the village green at the front. The bar food is good and reasonably priced, and there's also a restaurant. The beer is excellent, and the atmosphere is as warm and friendly as you could wish.

The pub dates back to the sixteenth century; its mellow brick and moss-covered roof make it seem as rooted in the village as the tree that shelters it, and, like most classic country pubs, it is the focus of village life. Inside are a series of low-beamed interconnecting rooms around a central bar. You can play darts, dominoes, pool, crib or shove ha'penny, sit around and chat or even wait for the 'grey lady'; like many other pubs, the Bledlow Lions has a resident pub ghost. She appears in the cellars or in an upstairs passageway, but seems to be entirely friendly.

If your intellect has now, temporarily, got the better of your appetite, head west through the pleasant town of Thame towards the cerebral delights of Oxford. If not, turn south and go in search of Stoke Row or other, less intellectual, but no less pleasant delights of the Chilterns.

When your wanderings have finally led you to Oxford, it would be a pity not to spend some time drinking in the architectural delights (and a few of the pubs too – best is the hard-to-find, but excellent Turf). Then head out past Woodstock, perhaps pausing to look at Blenheim Palace, home of the Churchills. If you go straight on to Stratford from there, however, without making a small diversion to Great Tew, you will miss one of the most

beautiful English villages and perhaps the most perfect example of a traditional village inn to be found anywhere.

The village lies to the north of the A34 Woodstock to Chipping Norton road (follow the sign to The Tews). You can also reach it from the A361 Banbury to Chipping Norton or A423 Banbury to Oxford roads. Great Tew was, until recently, the property of an eccentric Lord of the Manor, who kept the rents as low as 50 pence a week, but who also kept the village resolutely unimproved. Though this retained the traditional character of the village, it did mean that several of the houses were in imminent danger of collapse, and the end of that particular era may have come just in time. If the setting is perfect, a cluster of thatched, honey-coloured Cotswold stone buildings nestling around the village green, the jewel is undoubtedly the Falkland Arms. In summer, the thatch is almost smothered in a cloud of wisteria and the pub is the sort that makes expatriate Britons in the arid wastes of Saudi Arabia cry themselves to sleep at night.

The bar has a superb ingle-nook fireplace, stone-flagged floors worn smooth by centuries of use, high-backed settles, oak panels and beams, gleaming brassware and a ceiling covered with old beer mugs and jugs. The bar is tiny but its four china handpumps dispense more different traditional ales in a year than any other pub in Britain, and you can also buy English country wines, clay pipes

The Falkland Arms
Licensees: John and Hazel Milligan
Great Tew, Oxfordshire
☎ Great Tew (060 883) 653
11.30-2.30; 6-11. Closed Monday lunchtime in winter.

Donnington Best Bitter; Hook Norton Best Bitter; Theakston XB; Wadworth 6X; and a constantly-changing range of Guest Beers

Lunchtime & evening food (until 9). Accommodation. Families welcome. Garden.

The Falkland Arms, Great Tew, probably one of Britain's prettiest village pubs

as well as many different kinds of snuff.

The food is as traditional as the beer – English cheese, game pie, steak and ale pie, pork in cider. Eat your fill, drink a couple of pints from the often mind-boggling range of beers on offer, always including the two local breweries Hook Norton and Donnington, then spend the night in a four-poster bed in one of the three guest rooms – if that is not the perfect way to end the day I'll move to a tower block in Birmingham!

When you awake you will find yourself looking out over a quite superb English village, and after a hearty breakfast you will be ready to face whatever hardships life can throw at you.

Shakespeare Country lies to the south of Birmingham. Unfortunately Birmingham seems to embody the worst of the post-war city developments, with ugly tower blocks, and motorways cutting through the countryside. The city is probably worth a brief visit, if only to dispel any cosy, Cotswold-inspired notions that England consists of nothing but a series of impossibly pretty villages, but my route will not take you there. Follow me and I'll lead you past Stratford-upon-Avon (where the essential oasis in a sea of troubles is the White Swan, better known as the Dirty Duck) and through several Shakespeare Country classics, before turning back towards Oxford for an evening meal to remember at the George & Dragon at Chacombe.

All that comes later, however, for now the route is westward through a sea of Cotswold villages, each more beguilingly beautiful than the last, and each with its own thatched gem of a pub begging to be investigated; after an hour or two of the Cotswolds you long for the subtle charms of Birmingham or Slough just to restore a sense of balance.

From Great Tew the route passes through Chipping Norton and on to the north of Stow-on-the-Wold, where the first stop of the day beckons, the Fox at Broadwell, and you can renew acquaintance with an old friend, Donnington Bitter.

Take the A436 from Chipping Norton to Stow-on-the-Wold, and turn right three miles after the junction with the A44. Broadwell can also be reached by turning right from the A429 Stow to Moreton-in-Marsh road. Broadwell is yet another ridiculously pretty Cotswold village, with the pub, and its two labrador dogs, looking out over the village green.

The Fox Inn
Licensees: Denis & Debbie Harding
Broadwell, Moreton-in-Marsh, Gloucestershire
☎ Cotswold (0451) 30212
10-2.30; 6-11

Donnington BB, SBA; Weston Cider

Accommodation. Lunchtime & evening food (not Tuesday & Sunday evening); booking is recommended. Garden. Families welcome at lunchtime.

The Fox at Broadwell, a country local, with a friendly welcome

There's a beer garden at the back, where you can play the ancient pub game of 'Aunt Sally', excellent beer dispensed straight from the casks stillaged behind the bar and good home-made food which includes a traditional Sunday lunch. If you want to be sure of a meal, it may be wise to book. There's a blazing log fire in winter, and in the bar a stuffed squirrel apparently nesting at the top of a wooden pillar!

What really makes this pub a classic, as so often, is the people who run it. Denis and Debbie Harding are friendly and welcoming, running a fine pub which provides a great social life for its regulars and a fund of happy memories for its visitors.

On your way on towards Stratford, take the time for a small detour to nearby Upper Swell just off the B4077 west of Stow-on-the-Wold and have a look at the beautiful Donnington Brewery – with its Cotswold stone buildings reflected in a lake. If you're there when the cherry blossom is in bloom, the sight will take your breath away – you may need to go on to the Plough Inn at Ford and drink another pint of Donnington Bitter while you recover!

The Plough is yet another of England's 'oldest' inns and was originally an old Court House. The cellar was the gaol, and in one bar you can still see what is left of the stocks. Behind the front door is a 'bars up' – a stout piece of wood that pulls from the wall to

The Plough
Licensees: Les & Ann Carter
Ford, Gloucestershire
☎ Stanton (038 673) 215
10.30-2.30; 5.30-11

Donnington XXX, BB, SBA

Accommodation. Lunchtime & evening food. Families welcome. Music most evenings.

The mellow Cotswold-stone walls of the Plough at Ford

The Donnington Brewery. In an idyllic setting such as this, how could the beer be anything but delicious?

secure the door. Originally used to keep the lawless out and the law-abiding in, you may be tempted to try to reverse its use as closing time approaches, keeping the law at bay while you finish your drink, though the landlord is unlikely to look on your efforts with favour.

On the front of the Plough is a plaque claimed to have been engraved by the hand of William Shakespeare himself. Another carries the inscription:

This plough hangs high,
And hinders none,
So refresh and pay,
And travel on.

There is every incentive to accept the invitation, whoever actually issued it, for the pub is that much over-worked cliché, a gem. Flagstone floors, beams, stone walls, log fires, hops hanging over the bar and locals and strangers alike revelling in the character and atmosphere of a Great British pub. The Plough serves breakfast from 7 a.m. but if you don't make it until lunchtime, you can get one of the most delicious and attractively presented ploughman's lunches around – good English cheese, fresh-baked bread and a fine salad. If the weather is fine, there is a sun-trap garden and wooden benches just outside the inn. If you are enjoying yourself too much to leave there are guest bedrooms.

The next country classic on our route lies at the heart of an area almost as strongly linked with fruit growing as the Garden of England, the Vale of Evesham.

Bretforton is three miles east of Evesham, just off the B4035, and the pub we are travelling to is the Fleece.

There is a noble tradition in British pubs of indomitable women licensees, who rule over their pubs with a rod of iron, reigning supreme for decades, and who are remembered with respect and, more remarkably, with great affection. One of the most indomitable of all was Lola Taplin. Her family had owned the Fleece Inn at Bretforton for over 500 years and she ran it single-handed for the last thirty years of her long life, until her death in 1977 at the age of eighty-three.

It is said that she never let her customers forget that they were drinking in her family home and not just any old public house, and any who forgot their manners would be out on their ears in very quick time.

On her death, Lola Taplin left the inn, its magnificent contents and its gardens to the National Trust on condition that it continued to be run as an unspoilt country pub.

Originally a medieval farmhouse, the Fleece was converted to an inn in 1848 by Henry Byrd, Ms Taplin's great-grandfather. The interior and the furniture and ornaments used by the family remain as they were in the nineteenth century. The farm dairy became the brewhouse, producing beer and cider for the inn, and reminders of both these uses can be seen in the room still known as The Brewhouse, though the last home-produced beer was brewed over fifty years ago.

Off this room is the 'Dugout', once the farmhouse pantry, and still containing the coffin-like table in which dough was placed to 'prove', free from draughts. The pub's other room, once the farm kitchen, contains a stunning, and world famous, collection of pewter. Legend has it that the collection was left by Oliver Cromwell in return for gold and silver plate taken to pay the parliamentary armies during the Civil War.

In this room and the Brewhouse, 'witch-marks' can still be seen. To ward off evil spirits, charms were hung over doors and windows, while circles (chosen because they have no corners in which spirits can hide) were chalked on hearths to prevent entry through the chimney. The marks in the Brewhouse are indented into the stone through centuries of daily chalking.

You can find furniture and artefacts that are as interesting in a museum, but you will not find a family home preserved over centuries, where you can eat, drink good beer, or sit outside in the shade of an old thatched barn, anywhere but at the Fleece. Before you travel

Opposite: The pewter displayed in the Pewter Room at the Fleece, Bretforton, is reputed to have been left by Oliver Cromwell

The Fleece Inn
Licensees: Dan & Nora Davies
The Cross, Bretforton, nr Evesham, Hereford & Worcester
☎ Evesham (0386) 831173
10.30-2.30; 6-11

Hook Norton Best Bitter; M & B Brew XI; Marston Pedigree

Lunchtime & evening food. Families welcome. Garden.

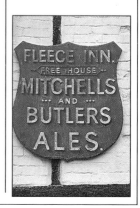

The Plough at Shenstone, only a few miles from the urban West Midlands, yet everything a rural local pub should be

on, drink a toast to Henry Byrd for making the Fleece into one of the finest pubs in Britain and to Lola Taplin and the National Trust for keeping it that way.

Leaving the Fleece is a good moment for a temporary parting of the ways. A myriad of Shakespearian delights await those who wish to have a look at Stratford. Those built of sterner stuff will pass up the enchantment of Anne Hathaway's cottage and even the Dirty Duck in exchange for a spell in the epitome of a good rural local pub, plus the chance to visit the oddest pub in the whole of Britain.

You will find Shenstone just off the A450, three miles south-east of Kidderminster, and the Plough at Shenstone, one of eight pubs owned by the tiny Daniel Batham brewery, is everything a good rural local should be. There are three bars, each with a distinct clientele – a few minutes sampling the atmosphere (and the superb Batham beer) should sort out which one best suits your mood on any particular occasion. One thing you can be sure of: though you arrive as a stranger, you won't be made to feel you're intruding.

The atmosphere, like the pub, is warm and friendly, and you can enjoy one of life's simple pleasures – a relaxed conversation round the bar which may wander over topics as diverse as sport, vegetable growing, the state of the nation or even the meaning of life. Despite its proximity to Britain's monument to motorway madness, there is no concession to Birmingham tastes at the Plough; it is

The Plough
Licensees: Edward & Marjorie Rose
Shenstone, Hereford & Worcester
☎ Chaddesley Corbett (056 283) 340
10-2.30; 7-10.30
(11 Friday & Saturday)

Batham Bitter, Delph Strong Ale (winter); Weston Cider

Food: snacks only. Families welcome. Garden.

a country pub, not a suburban roadhouse.

The licensees, Edward and Marjorie, have presided over the Plough for more than thirty years and you have the happy feeling of being a guest at an impromptu party of theirs rather than a paying customer. The beer regrettably isn't free, but it is very reasonably priced. In summer, enjoy it outside among the flowers; in winter, settle in by the fire or chance your arm at a game of darts. Be warned, though: the daughter of the house has ambitions to play professionally!

From Shenstone, head north, skirting the western edge of Birmingham and unearth the weird and wonderful world of the Crooked House. The pub is signposted as the Crooked House off the B4176 a mile east of the A491. You approach past an old quarry, down a winding private road lined with flowers. There are woods and meadows beyond the pub – you have to pinch yourself to remember that you are near the heart of one of the most heavily industrialised areas in Britain.

The attraction here is not just the unexpected West Midlands arcadia, but the pub itself. A landslip and mining subsidence have created a bizarre building, tilted 15° out of the vertical, with doors, windows, floors and furniture all at crazy angles.

As you step through the door, you find yourself staggering as your mind tries to make

The Crooked House (The Glynne Arms)
Licensees: Gary & Dawn Ensor
Off Himley Road, Gornal, nr Dudley, West Midlands
☎ Dudley (038) 238583
11-2.30; 6-10.30

Banks's Mild, Bitter

Food: bar snacks only.
Families welcome. Garden.

The Crooked House at Himley, probably the strangest pub in Britain, where even the teetotal feel drunk

sense of the conflicting information the eyes are sending, and to open the door into the lounge bar requires a fair degree of strength as the slope is against you. A grandfather clock is secured to the wall by a metal band, the doors and the windows lean in opposite directions, and there is not a true vertical or horizontal to be seen. A bottle laid on its side on a table disconcertingly rolls 'uphill' – you can feel distinctly drunk without even touching the beer.

There is a terraced area at the front of the pub, surrounded by a white wooden fence, where you can sit and try and make sense of the building, once roofed with wooden shingles, now roofed with slates after an unfortunate incident with a spark from the fire! This pub, at least, has no pretensions to being the oldest in Britain, but it is certainly the most unusual by a crooked mile.

The Crooked House is as close to Birmingham as we are going to get, for our road now leads back through the Cotswolds, calling in at one more pub which stands as a testament to another extraordinary landlady. The Case Is Altered at Five Ways is the sort of pub that is full of atmosphere, even when you're the only person in there.

Approach the pub from the A41 at the junction with the A4177, and you will find it a short distance west along Rowington Road. If you're looking for space invaders, juke boxes or fruit machines, you're wasting your time. If you're looking for a timeless example of a classic country pub, you've found it.

At the front is a tiny yard with a square stone table, shaded by a tree. Inside are three rooms. One, the lounge, is opened only at weekends, when you can admire the carved oak furniture, copper jugs and a fine etched glass lamp. There is a pre-decimal bar-billiards table in the room leading to the main bar, where the glow of a fire, warm brick and tile, and an atmosphere of peace, quiet and contentment make it very easy to forget the rest of the world and pass a few hours chatting or just taking your ease.

The Case Is Altered owes much of its present character to a landlady who rejoiced in the splendid name of Mercedes Griffiths, known by those familiar or brave enough as 'Merc'. Like Lola Taplin at the Fleece, she was a formidable character who brooked no misbehaviour, but she is remembered with affection as well as respect. It is now run by another woman of Welsh ancestry – Mary Gwendoline Jones – and her partner William Saltmarsh.

The Case Is Altered
Licensees: Mary Gwendoline Jones & William Saltmarsh
Five Ways, Rowington Road, Haseley Knob, Hatton, Warwickshire
☎ Haseley Knob (092 687) 206
11-2.30; 6-11

Ansells Mild, Bitter; Flowers Original

No food. Small garden. Families welcome.

Opposite: The Rose & Crown at Ratley, seen from the churchyard. The pub was originally built to house the workers constructing the church

The Case is Altered at Five Ways . . . with a delightfully traditional interior

There are, inevitably, two versions of the origin of the pub's unusual name. The more probable is that it stems from the Spanish *Casa Alta* (the High House) a name brought back by returning soldiers from the Peninsula War. The fact that there are several other pubs of the same name around the country lends credence to this, but Mercedes' preferred explanation was that it arose from her struggles to get a spirits licence.

Back in the 19th century, when she owned it, the pub was a beer-house, consisting only of the present bar. The bar-billiards room was a separate cottage, and the lounge was a bakehouse. An application for a spirits licence was turned down on the grounds that the pub was too small. Undaunted, Mercedes set about acquiring the cottage and the bakehouse and, having done so, she went back to the magistrates. As the pub was now much bigger, the case was altered; she got her licence and the pub got a new name.

You may be beginning to feel surfeited with excellent pubs, but two Shakespeare Country classics remain that no self-respecting pub lover should miss. There are thousands of pubs around the country that have been 'improved' to the point of extinction at the hands of insensitive architects, designers and landlords, so let us be grateful for the wisdom of the owners of the Rose & Crown at Ratley, who have com-

*The sign of the Rose &
Crown at Ratley, perfectly in
keeping with the character and
quality of the pub itself*

pleted a drastic, and highly successful 'de-modernisation' of the pub, restoring it to a fair approximation of its original twelfth-century condition.

The pub was built to house the workers constructing the lovely church nearby. It's fairly well off the main tourist routes, so you can usually enjoy the lovely garden and the bar with its beams, ingle-nook fireplace, stone walls and flagstone floors without fighting your way through the tourist hordes.

Ratley is five miles north-west of Banbury, just off the B4086, in the valley below Edge Hill, one of the few hills within easy reach of Oxford. It is notable not only for its stunning views over the surrounding flatlands, but for being the site of the first great battle of the Civil War. Edgehill, the massive battle of 1642 between the Cavaliers and the Roundheads, still provides farmers ploughing their lands with an occasional relic – a helmet, a piece of armour or a cannonball.

As far as one can tell, Charles I neither hid in the roof of the Rose & Crown, nor in any of the neighbouring trees, but despite, or possibly because of this, the pub is definitely worth getting off the well-worn tourist track to find.

If you have stuck faithfully to your task, the sun should now be sinking in the West, you'll be tired of driving round looking at pubs, and you're probably ravenous. Keep the faith! The day's biggest treat is

The Rose & Crown
Licensee: William Castle
Ratley, Warwickshire
☎ Edge Hill (029 587) 636
12-2.30; 7-11

Donnington BB, SBA

Lunchtime food. Garden.
Families welcome.

*The George & Dragon at
Chacombe, a 'nouvelle
cuisine-free zone', where the
range of food is as extensive as
the landlord himself*

yet to come – dinner at the George & Dragon at Chacombe.

Chacombe is two miles north-east of Banbury, and can be reached by turning right off the A361 or left off the B4525. The George & Dragon is at the heart of the village, where every village pub should be. Dick East, the landlord, is a Falstaffian character as jolly and cheerful as the pub he keeps. A glance at the excellent menu he offers might suggest that this is one of those places that is actually a licensed restaurant masquerading as a pub. Don't be fooled, for the George & Dragon is a fine local pub, which also just happens to lay on some of the most memorable pub food you could wish for.

Everything on the menu is fresh and cooked to order. The bar snacks are excellent, the dinners (served Wednesday to Saturday, and if you have not booked, you are likely to go hungry) are better still. The rules of the house inscribed on the menu give you a fair idea of Dick's cuisine – and his humour. 'Rule 4: This establishment has been designated a Nouvelle Cuisine free zone. Rule 5: No bloody Lymeswold!' With dishes like Fillet of Brill with Pickled Walnuts, or Rabbit with Red Peppers and Zucchine on offer, who cares about the bloody Lymeswold? The illustration on the menu also has a nice reversal – in this George & Dragon picture the patron saint of England is about to be devoured by a happy-looking dragon with a smile on his face, a knife and fork in his hands and a bottle of damsel sauce!

After Dick took over the pub his first culinary ventures were greeted with a fair amount of diffidence by the pub regulars, but his enthusiasm and the aromas drifting through from the kitchen began to weave their magic spells; his local customers are now his most enthusiastic supporters.

Dick's culinary spectaculars come once a month on a Saturday night, however, when he lays on a banquet that may run to twenty courses featuring the farmhouse cuisine of a particular area of the world. Thailand, Gujarat, New Zealand, Sicily, Russia and Peking are among many to receive the East treatment, after long hours of research and long journeys for fresh ingredients.

Such is the fame of these nights that the waiting list extends to over a year, though there is a reserve list in case of late withdrawals. If you can't wait a year, it is worth going anyway to enjoy the beer, the atmosphere and the sheer vitality and humour of a classic country landlord running a classic country pub.

The George & Dragon
Licensees: Dick & Lorna East
Silver Street, Chacombe, Northamptonshire
☎ Banbury (0295) 710602
11.30-2.30; 6-11
(Restaurant licence)

Draught Bass; Donnington XXX, BB; Guest beers

Lunchtime & evening food (dinner Wednesday to Saturday). Garden. Families welcome.

The sign of the George & Dragon at Chacombe; book early, or go hungry

To the West Country

'We were in the tame and gentle hills of Devon . . . Here the rain made the landscape mild, and sheep grazed near flowering hedgerows, and from the railway tracks to the horizon there were ten shades of green.'

THE KINGDOM BY THE SEA
PAUL THEROUX

Our route to the West Country takes in some of Britain's most ancient and most heavily visited sites. In every region the pleasure of visiting the country classic pubs is greatly enhanced by doing so out of the main tourist season; in the case of the West Country, it is absolutely essential. There is nothing more wearisome than sitting in a traffic jam for hours on end for the privilege of standing in a queue at the local ancient monument and an even longer one at the bar of the local pub.

Drive down past Oxford and take the A420 towards Swindon. You will travel down the Vale of the White Horse, so named for the vast, 360 foot long chalk carving of the Uffington White Horse. You can also visit Wayland's Smithy and walk part of the ancient Ridge Way, perhaps all the way past Liddington Castle and Barbury Castle to Avebury, a stone circle larger even than Stonehenge. Nearby are the neolithic mound at Silbury Hill and the West Kennet Long Barrow.

Travelling on south across Salisbury Plain, you can see Stonehenge on the way to Salisbury. After a look at Old Sarum, abandoned in 1217 when New Sarum (Salisbury) became the cathedral city, head south to the coast. Our destination is on the inappropriately named Isle of Purbeck, which is no more than a peninsula enclosing Poole Harbour. Take the road round through Wareham to Corfe Castle, built by Edward I in 1280, now in ruins, but still dominating the village huddling around it. In the village you will find a pub called the Fox.

The Fox is a tiny old pub, remarkably unspoilt by its proximity to the centre of the Corfe Castle tourist trap. At the height of the season, the town's best-known pub, the Greyhound, spectacularly placed beneath the gaunt and forbidding ruins of the castle, is virtually unapproachable because of the crowds. A short walk round the corner and up the steep street brings you to the parlour pub, the Fox, opposite the church.

You will not lose sight of the castle; there are good views of it from the small garden at the back of the pub. Walk straight into the parlour from the street and this really is home from home, with a large, dominating oak table, seats and wall benches and service through a hatch. If you prefer, you can go down a few steps into the servery, where the beer comes frothing straight from casks behind the counter. Beyond the servery is another small room, though locals seem to

The Fox
Licensee: Annette Brown
West Street, Corfe Castle, Dorset
☎ Corfe Castle (0929) 480449
10.30-2.30; 6-11

EST.ᴰ 1742

Whitbread Strong Country Bitter, Pompey Royal

Lunchtime & evening food. Garden

prefer to stand in the passage to drink and chat.

The pub lunches are excellent and remarkable value for money in a town where prices dig deep into unwary pockets. Locally caught crab with salad is particularly good value, and there are sandwiches, ploughmans, savoury pancakes, pâté and salads as well.

The Fox has been in the same family for decades, and on Shrove Tuesday the Company of Marblers and Stonecutters meet and regale themselves there, honouring a centuries-old Purbeck custom of presenting the Lord of the Manor with a pound of peppercorns. After the presentation they have to prove

The Fox, not the best-known pub in Corfe Castle, but certainly the best find

their sobriety by running across the road holding their pints without spilling a drop.

The next classic pub, the Square & Compass at Worth Matravers, is close at hand, just off the busy Corfe Castle to Swanage road, but it is a journey through time to this unspoilt, bucolic old pub, rightly described by the *Good Beer Guide* as 'a bastion of Purbeck'. Take the B3069 off the A351 and watch for the signs to the village.

The Square & Compass has been licensed for 260 years, and the building, formerly a farm, dates back to the 'Domesday Book'. The name stems from the time when quarrymen were busy in the Isle of Purbeck, and the pub probably has not changed a jot since then.

Beer comes straight from casks behind a hatch in a servery. There is a flagstoned corridor, replete with local fossils and other

The Square & Compass
Licensee: Ray Newman
Worth Matravers, Dorset
☎ Worth Matravers (092 943) 229
10.30-2.30; 6-11

ESTᴰ 1742

Whitbread Strong Country Bitter, Pompey Royal; Bulmers Cider

Garden. Families welcome.

curios, and a plain, occasionally sun-filled parlour with wall benches, old tables, local pictures and a low ceiling. There are no fruit machines, video games or piped music, but traditional pub games include shove ha'penny, dominoes, darts and cribbage.

The pub is a small, white-painted building, with seats in the spacious area at the front, a free-standing pub sign and chickens strutting and pecking on the grass and gravel. The views are magnificent, with the sea dappling in the distance beyond the cliffs off St Alban's Head.

The Drewe Arms
Licensee: Mabel Mudge
Drewsteignton, Devon
☎ Drewsteignton (0647) 21224
10.30-2.30; 6-10.30

EST.ᴰ 1742

Flowers IPA; Whitbread Strong Country Bitter; Bulmers Traditional Cider

Food: sandwiches only. Families welcome.

We are leaving Purbeck behind us now, heading west along the coast, but with a few detours to look at some of Dorset's many other attractions along the way. Follow the delightfully named River Piddle up from Wareham and you will come to Tolpuddle, a key site in British labour history, as the home of the Tolpuddle Martyrs. Just to the west is Puddletown; the nearby Waterston Manor was used by Thomas Hardy as the model for Bathsheba's house in *Far from the Madding Crowd*.

The whole area is rich in associations with Hardy, and lovers of his Wessex tales will want to visit Dorchester, calling on the way at Higher Bockhampton, where Hardy was born. South of Dorchester is Maiden Castle, one of the finest Iron Age hill-forts in Britain, besieged by the invading Romans in 43 BC.

From Dorchester, wander west along the coast, stopping when the mood takes you: perhaps at Lyme Regis, granted its royal suffix by Edward I and boasting the highest cliff on the southern coast; perhaps at the enticingly titled village of Beer. Cross into Devon and keep on through Exeter, its county town, sheltering in the shadow of Rougemont Castle and the twin-towered cathedral. Pick up the A30 beyond Exeter, turn south at the sign to Cheriton Bishop and follow the back roads to the village of Drewsteignton.

The approach to the village is along a single-track road, winding between hedges which sometimes tower above the road. Up the hill at the heart of the village is a little square with the village shop, a fine Norman church and the thatched Drewe Arms, originally built to house the workers constructing the church.

A rustic archway over the entrance to the pub is smothered in honeysuckle. Step inside and you have the feeling of entering another era. The Drewe Arms has been in the hands of the same family for over one hundred years,

Opposite: The Square & Compass, Worth Matravers, looks out across its lawns to the sea

and the present licensee, Mrs Mudge, known as 'Auntie Mabel' to all her locals, has lived there since 1919. At ninety-one years of age, she may be Britain's oldest landlady, and, though she has help from younger members of her family and from stripling staff barely two-thirds her age, Mrs Mudge is still very definitely in charge.

There is a grandfather clock in the entrance hall; off the hall is a small room rich in the patina of age, with plain wooden tables and benches right round the walls. It does not appear to have been altered in any way since the Mudge family took it over. There is no bar; drinks are carried through from the servery. A back room houses comfortable armchairs and a piano, brought into use for lively social nights. There was a big party for 'Auntie Mabel's' ninetieth birthday; her one hundredth promises to be quite a night. You can play darts, if you wish, but the main function of the pub is to act as the focus of the village, the place to sit and chat. One of life's simple, under-rated pleasures is just to sit by a fireside on a cold winter's day and talk; the Drewe Arms is an ideal place to indulge in it.

Mrs Mudge can still remember horses and traps being despatched to the station at Moretonhampstead six miles away, to collect tourists staying at the inn. Those days are now long gone, the station and the railway line are closed and the Drewe Arms no longer offers accommodation, though the pub is as busy in summer as ever. It was originally named the Druids Arms; the name was changed when Castle Drogo was built early this century, Drogo or Dru being the name of the local landowner at the time of the Domesday survey.

The road out of Drewsteignton to the picturesque small market town of Chagford passes Castle Drogo, Lutyens' extraordinary 'baronial hall' constructed in granite in 1910. Now owned by the National Trust, it is a fine example of the grandiose style which became Lutyens' hallmark throughout the colonies.

Chagford was one of the 'stannary' towns which, centuries ago, administered Dartmoor's tin mines. Taking any of the small roads to the south you will eventually reach the B3212 road across the moor. The route via Manaton to Widecombe will take you past Becky Falls and the Yarner Wood nature reserve and affords some splendid views. If you prefer the bleaker terrain of the upper moor, then it pays to turn towards Princetown and turn off the road two miles short of

Rugglestone Inn
Licensee: G. E. Lamb
Widecombe-in-the-Moor,
Devon
12-2.30; 7-11

Draught Bass

No food. Garden.

The Rugglestone Inn, nestling in Widecombe-in-the-Moor

Postbridge to find Grimspound. This bronze-age settlement is said to have been the inspiration for Conan Doyle's *Hound of the Baskervilles*.

Widecombe-in-the-Moor attracts tourists by the charabanc load who come to buy souvenirs of Uncle Tom Cobbleigh and all, and gaze at not a lot. The church is dedicated to St Pancras, and at the height of the summer his more famous London station will appear less populous. To appreciate Widecombe one has to see it from afar, nestling in the valley between the high tors, tranquil and assured. Its most beautiful secret is without doubt the Rugglestone Inn.

To find the Rugglestone, go to the church and take the lane out of the village signposted 'Ye Olde Glebe House'. Four hundred yards on, you will come to a bend in the road, and on your left is the old stone building with its babbling brook. The tiny inn sign against the front wall is the only indication of its function.

I first found it in mid-winter a few years back. There had been a funeral at the church and soon after twelve o'clock a small band of old boys of the village joined us in the quiet public bar, settling round the fire. For what seemed like an hour they sat in silence and thereby silenced my little party. I pondered the meaning of life and the uses of black ties until one of their number turned to the chap at the end and said, 'You'll be the oldest one coming here now then Jack.' The atmosphere broke and the wake began.

Is this the only traditional moors pub left on Dartmoor? The main bar room has a few settles, one or two tables, a simple fireplace and no bar, just a door behind which some casks are stillaged. The front room is little more than a table with a half-dozen chairs. For obvious reasons, this is not an inn which goes out of its way to attract the coach parties, but nevertheless the locals make visitors feel welcome.

Parking is non-existent, so it is best to walk from the village. If you prefer all mod cons the village's other pub, a fourteenth-century freehouse, will oblige with good facilities.

Lydford Castle towers over the Castle Inn. The Castle has a grim history: 'First hang and draw; then hear the case by Lydford Law' was a saying inspired by Judge Jefferies' 'Bloody Assizes'

From the stark realities of the Rugglestone, a journey across the moor to Lydford will bring you to the sublime extravagance of the Castle Inn. To travel from Widecombe to Two Bridges, head either for Postbridge to the north or Ponsworthy to the south and then join either of the two roads which traverse the heart of the moor. The barren landscape, the rocky outcrops and the occasional herds of wild ponies are essential viewing for those unfamiliar with the area.

Beyond Two Bridges is Princetown, the home of Dartmoor Prison. Seen in a grey mist and light drizzle, it is a greater deterrent to crime than any hangman's noose. Take the B3357 past Merrivale, then head north towards Okehampton. Exactly half-way between Tavistock and Okehampton on the western border of the moor sits Lydford, one

Castle Inn
Proprietors: David & Susan Grey
Lydford, Devon
☎ Lydford (082 282) 242
11-2.30; 6-10.30
(11 Friday, Saturday & summer)

Ushers Best Bitter, Founders Ale

Lunchtime & evening food. Restaurant. Accommodation. Families welcome. Garden.

of the prettiest of Devon's many splendid villages. Next to the twelfth-century castle, an old stannary prison, you will find the inn.

Built in 1550, its plain white walls give little clue to the stunning interior. Slate floors and stone walls house a superb collection of high-back settles, including a rare hooded example in the passage by the snug bar. The walls are adorned with lacy plates, copper kettles and curios from every era. The 'Lydford pennies', bronze and silver coins from the reign of Ethelred the Unready, can be seen by the bar. The Hogarth prints are originals, as are the sturdy beams. The fireplace boasts Norman scrolls on its stonework, which was

The beautiful exterior of the St Kew Inn is matched by its warm and welcoming interior

original to the inn, but probably pinched by the builders from the castle next door.

As if the furnishings were not impressive enough, the hospitality excels. 'Probably the best Steak and Kidney Pudding in the South West', an advertiser might have it; it is one of a wide range of bar snacks, all home-made. The more expensive restaurant mirrors the quality. Rooms are old, comfortable and excellent value, especially for winter breaks. Families are welcome in the delightful snug bar at the back, or in the lounge bar if eating. Sunday lunch draws in the local farming community.

Leaving Lydford village, the route passes Lydford Gorge, a National Trust area with over a mile of waterfalls and rocky glades. A few miles south on the road past Brent Tor you will spot a faintly ludicrous thirteenth-century church, St Michael de Rude's, perched on a rocky outcrop in the middle of nowhere. The short climb makes for an excellent way of working off Mrs Grey's delicious cuisine.

Eventually you will reach the Tavistock–Launceston road and should take the right turn to Milton Abbot and Cornwall. Past Launceston you will skirt the northern edge of Bodmin Moor along the A395 in the direction of Camelford. The legend of King Arthur is big business on this part of Cornwall's north coast. A mile before you reach Camelford you will find Slaughterbridge, which bears witness to the single relic that may give substance to the legend. It is here that Arthur is said to have fought his final battle with Mordred. It is close to the River Camel, as in Camelot, and in a grotto nearby there is a stone bearing a Latin inscription which reads, with the eye of faith, 'Here lies Latinus, son of Arthorus'.

Eight miles beyond Camelford on the Wadebridge road you will come to the village of St Kew Highway. Just beyond the village on your right is the signpost to St Kew village itself, one and a half miles off the main road.

The St Austell brewery owns many a quaint Cornish inn, but the St Kew Inn is the jewel in the crown. It is the centrepiece of the village. Its granite façade is at its most impressive on an autumn night of no moon: simply lit, austere but welcoming.

The parlour bar with its roaring log fire, the meat hooks hanging from the ceiling, the worn slate floor and the indescribable 'lived-

St Kew Inn
Licensee: Harry Arkley
St Kew, Cornwall
☎ St Mabyn (020 884) 259
10.30-2.30; 6-10.30
(11 Friday, Saturday & summer)

St Austell Tinners Ale, Hicks Special

Food: bar snacks only at lunchtime, full menu evenings. No food on Sunday and sometimes no food Monday to Wednesday in winter. Families welcome only before 8.30 and if eating. No carrycots. No dogs.

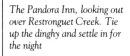

The Pandora Inn, looking out over Restronguet Creek. Tie up the dinghy and settle in for the night

in' look warms the heart of even the most hardened pub-goer. The wooden casks stillaged behind the bar-front and the excellent ale served straight from the barrel make this a superb experience, out of season. The old world dining-room and the newly added lounge would excel elsewhere. The 'new' lounge is all slate and stone, of course, and the open fire works hard.

Despite the wonderful atmosphere, it is the steaks that bring many people here. Quite simply they are the best you will ever sample in England. Cooked in a special skillet, the kitchen staff sworn to secrecy, they arrive perfect every time. Be warned that even out of season you will wait an hour to be served; and in July and August, well, sad to say, it is hardly worth bothering.

If you are in the neighbourhood of St Kew between October and May, then treat yourself to a splendid evening; and try the smoked mackerel with horseradish for starters.

There is no doubting that Cornwall has a glut of first-rate pubs and, alas, there is no room to include more than the cream of them here. Our next scheduled stop takes us across central Cornwall to the south coast just beyond Truro. After Wadebridge you may like to take a detour north to the beautiful fishing port of Padstow, with its working harbour and sea-food tanks. A pint at the London Inn is worthwhile too. Alternatively, later on your route you may like to leave the A390 short of Truro and head towards St Mawes, crossing the River Fal at King Harry's ferry. If you do, then seek out the Roseland Inn at Philleigh for a bite to eat and a fine glass of ale.

Whichever route you take, beyond Truro you will find yourself on the A394 Helston road. At Perranarworthal turn left towards Carclew. Restronguet is occasionally signposted and occasionally not. At the first unmarked cross-roads turn left, and after a mile you will come to another set. The tiny sign to Restronguet Passage on your left may or may not be visible. If you find yourself descending a narrow, winding, increasingly steep incline then you are on the right road!

The unique creekside setting of the Pandora Inn will come upon you suddenly. If you miss it you may find that you have inadvertently driven into the water. The Pandora has suffered the same fate as many a Cornish fisherman's haunt: it has been cleaned out and, God forbid, painted. Anyone who remembers this place as a smoky,

Pandora Inn
Licensees: Roger & Helen Hough
Restronguet Creek, Cornwall
☎ Falmouth (0326) 72678
10.30-2.30; 6-11

St Austell BB, Tinners Ale, Hicks Special; Draught Bass

Bar snacks lunchtime & evening. Restaurant Monday to Saturday (summer), Wednesday to Saturday (October to Easter).

dingy, cobwebbed and disreputable drinking establishment of a few years ago may be disappointed; but the Pandora remains a classic.

Licensees Roger and Helen Hough have highlighted its four distinct bars and have resisted any temptation to introduce noisy machines or background muzak. The fireplaces are still half-way up the wall in case of flood. The brass nautical relics shine as new. The beer comes from a temperature-controlled spick-and-span cellar which guarantees good quality even in the sweltering (?) summer months. The food is top rate and features a wide variety of home-made dishes in both the bars and the restaurant. Well behaved families are made more than welcome.

Outside, the riverside drinking area offers a panoramic view along the creek. The moorings are free during the day, and the £3 overnight charge is waived if the crew eat at the pub in the evening.

Some will miss the silt-soaked wellies and the blue language of the mucky smock brigade. The old range in the Bounty bar almost dazzles with its new sheen, but the Houghs have put a lot of thought and care into the Pandora, and as the white walls become more smoke-stained, who knows, the odd cobweb might return?

The road from Restronguet leads through the wooded hillsides to Penryn. Take the Falmouth road but turn right on to the winding back road past Constantine. You can visit a seal sanctuary in Gweek, where a largely volunteer workforce helps injured seals washed up on the Cornish coast recuperate ready for a return to the wild. Alternatively, drive on until you reach the St Keverne turning. A few miles up that road Mawgan will be signposted to the left. At the end of the village follow signs to Manaccan.

The New Inn is on the far side of the village. In the summer, the garden is a nice place to sit and sample the excellent ale straight from the barrels racked behind the bar and eat from Belinda Cullinan's extraordinary menu. Out of season, step inside on a cold evening and enjoy the pleasures of the English country pub at its finest.

Paddy Cullinan has the air of a retired spymaster from a Le Carré novel, though he assures me he is no such thing. His pub has the atmosphere of the squire's back parlour; one expects to see his slippers warming in the hearth by the family dog.

The old ingle-nook is impractical for the

New Inn
Licensees: Paddy & Belinda Cullinan
Manaccan, Cornwall
☎ Manaccan (032 623) 323
11-2.30; 6-10.30
(11 Friday & Saturday)

Devenish Bitter, Cornish Original

Lunchtime and evening food all week except Tuesday evening (October to Easter). Families welcome, though space is limited. Large garden.

Opposite: Beneath its thatched roof, the New Inn at Manaccan enjoys a perfect peaceful setting

small pub, so it acts as a romantic hidey-hole for quiet conversation and perhaps a candle-lit supper. The pub games are chess and backgammon. There is occasional background music, Radio 3 or the Sunday Service, but otherwise no noise invades the peaceful retreat.

Lovers of real lavatories will appreciate the ivy-clad gentlemen's outhouse, reminiscent of the playground bogs in an ancient prep school. Be warned that parking can be frenetic, even in winter.

If you visit Manaccan on a dark night and have a penchant for unreal experiences, then your route to Helston should include the telecommunications dishes on Goonhilly Downs. Rising from the downs like space-age windmills, they could be mistaken for leftover special effects from a Steven Spielberg movie.

During the daytime you can visit the nearby Flambards Aero Park, a professionally assembled museum of ancient flying machines, just down the road from the Royal Naval Air Station at Culdrose. On the site there is a meticulous replica of a Victorian high street featuring, amongst many other exhibits, a life-like reconstruction of an 1880s beer-house.

The road to Helston is well marked. As you enter the town, a glimpse of the road signs and street names brings to reality the idea that Cornish is an ancient tongue with no real connection with modern English. A few miles down the road in Penzance, they regularly elect councillors for the Cornish nationalist party.

Our final stop before heading 'up-country' again is one of the most famous pubs in all England – not that they consider themselves English here. At the turn of the century there were 20,000 pubs still brewing their own ale on the premises. Although around seventy-five home-brew pubs have been established in recent years, back in 1975 only four remained. The Blue Anchor was by far the oldest, and its beers were the most distinctive.

The building dates from 1400, when it was a monks' retreat and probably included a brewhouse. It became a pub around 1550. The sloping street has gulleys between the pavements and the roadway, which run like rivulets with the slightest rain. With its warren of rooms, the pub is quite large but remains first and foremost an ale-house.

The front bar is rowdy, the greeting for 'emmets' (ants = tourists) can be caustic, and the language runs as flavoursome as the

The Blue Anchor
Licensee: Sid Cannon
Coinagehall Street,
Helston, Cornwall
☎ Helston (0326) 562821
10.30-2.30; 6-10.30
(11 Friday & Saturday)

Blue Anchor Middle Bitter, Best Bitter, Special and/or Extra Special

Lunchtime and early evening snacks. No food Sunday. Families by permission.

'Crisp malting' at the Blue Anchor, Helston, produces some extraordinarily potent beer

pasties. The back room attracts the passing trade and a fair smattering of languid, pipe-smoking, Arran sweater and walking-boot types. The skittle alley at the back is as old as the pub itself and is used on Fridays for live music. The whole place breathes a boozy eccentricity.

If you ask Sid Cannon nicely he will usually show you the old brewhouse, visible above the back yard. The beers are potent brews, so beware. Even the ordinary bitter has an original gravity of 1050, which means that it matches the strength of most premium real ales. The Special and Extra Special are darker, sweeter beers, strictly for the experts.

There are legal children's rooms at the side of the pub, but parental supervision and licensee's assent are called for. The food is basic, but the pasties can be recommended.

The homely interior of the Blue Anchor at Helston

There is now a long drive to the north coast of Devon for the next classic pub. Along the way, one near-obligatory stopping point is Tintagel Castle, the legendary site of the birth of King Arthur. The castle is in a truly spectacular setting, almost torn in half by the force of the sea, with the castle gateway on the mainland and the great hall, reached by a causeway, on an island off the coast. There are also the remains of a great Celtic monastery. With Atlantic breakers crashing against the cliffs and the wind keening around you, the Arthurian legends seem far more real than when you are surrounded by the tawdry tourist tat in the village of Tintagel.

The whole coast of Devon and Cornwall is covered by the South West Peninsula Coast Path, at 515 miles the longest continuous path in Britain. If you feel energetic, join it for a few miles along the beautiful northern coastline, then drive on around the coast past Bude, which probably has the best surfing beaches in Britain, and Clovelly, a village with a steep, cobbled main street that is almost too pretty to be true. Continue through Barnstaple, following the A39 towards Lynton.

There are two ways to reach our next classic pub: either turn left at Blackmoor Gate and take the right turn signed to the Hunters Inn, or, more spectacularly, keep on the A39 and take the left turn past Parracombe running down the steep, rocky gorge of the Heddon Valley that leads to the Hunters Inn. The valley is one of the deepest in England and the mile-long footpath past the inn down to the sea is remarkable, the cliffs towering high above you on either side.

Behind the inn are three acres of gardens, with five lakes, full of ducks and geese, and peacocks wandering over the lawns. The original inn dated back centuries, but a fire at the end of the nineteenth century completely destroyed the old building. The present one was built in 'Swiss chalet style' because the Heddon Valley was widely known as 'the

The Hunters Inn
Licensee: Reed Evans
Heddon's Mouth,
Parracombe, Devon
☎ Parracombe (059 83) 230
11-2.30; 6-11

Draught Bass; Flowers Original; Golden Hill Exmoor Ale; Hunters Inn IPA; Samuel Whitbread Strong Ale; Hancocks Cider

Lunchtime & evening food. Restaurant. Accommodation. Families welcome. Large garden. Barbecues summer Tuesday nights. Coffee and afternoon tea served in summer.

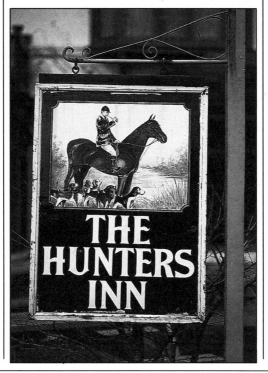

Switzerland of England'.

The Hunters is a very popular attraction in summer, sometimes almost smothered by coaches and cars. In winter the valley has much of the feeling captured in Blackmore's *Lorna Doone*; much more, in fact, than the real Doone Valley inland on Exmoor, which seems an inappropriately gentle setting for the notorious Doones.

A saddle hanging in the Hunters Inn, Parracombe. The walk down to the beach from the pub is spectacular

After emerging from the very private world of the Heddon Valley, our route picks up the A39 again and continues towards Lynton, though you may want to see one of the most unusual churches in Britain first. St Petrock's Church at Parracombe has remained completely unaltered for two centuries. A new church was built for the village in 1879; this one is officially redundant, but a perfect museum piece. There are hat pegs on the walls, benches for the less affluent, and draught-proofed boxes for the better off. The pulpit has three tiers and an elaborately decorated sounding board. At the back of the church are banks of pews, one with a panel removed so that the bass viol player could use his bow without banging his knuckles. The church must have been one of the last in Britain where the singing was led by musicians rather than an organist.

Lynton and Lynmouth are 'twin' towns separated by a six hundred foot cliff. An enterprising local character devised a two-car cable railway to link the towns, which is still in use today as a tourist attraction. Each car has a tank, and at the top the tank is filled with water, making the car heavy enough to haul up the one at the bottom as it descends. The tank of the ascending car being empty, the only power involved is that of gravity. Lynmouth is a lovely village standing at the head of the River Lyn, with lawns running down to the sea and a tiny harbour. The River Lyn is actually two streams, the East and West Lyn, which come together at the beautiful Watersmeet a few hundred yards inland.

The area is one of remarkable beauty, thickly wooded river valleys, rocky gorges and rushing water. In 1952 it was the scene of a terrible natural disaster, when the river, already swollen after weeks of rain, was fed by a cloudburst on Exmoor. The resultant torrent swept away rocks, trees and buildings and caused the death of thirty-four people. Lynmouth has been completely restored and the river, though untamed, should never again be able to wreak such havoc.

Heading east from Lynmouth, the road

climbs high on to the cliffs, giving superb sea views as it runs right along the cliff-edge. Descend into Porlock either by the main A39, which culminates in a one in four hill well served with escape roads and warning signs, or by a toll road, which takes an even more scenic route and avoids such a steep descent.

A few miles round the coast from Porlock, just past Minehead, Dunster Castle perches on a hilltop in a beautiful setting, looking down on the medieval village below. The Yarn Market, the church and the dovecot are all notable sights in a lovely and completely unspoilt village. Take the stiff walk up to the castle, which dates back to 1070, though the present building is largely seventeenth and nineteenth century. You can look out from the castle across superb views in all directions.

Further round the bay is Watchet, where Samuel Taylor Coleridge was inspired to write 'The Ancient Mariner'; it was written in a cottage in Nether Stowey, which you pass through on the way into Bridgwater. Just east of Bridgwater is the site of the battle of Sedgemoor, where Monmouth's rebellion came to grief in 1685. Sedgemoor is also the place where, in a ninth-century incident memorable to every schoolchild, King Alfred burnt the cakes.

Take the road east towards Glastonbury, where the tor topped by the tower of the fifteenth-century church of St Michael is a landmark for miles around in this flat plain. Here, once more, the Arthurian legends pervade the area; this is alleged to be Avalon, the island rising from the marshes all around, the place where Arthur is buried.

On the way to Glastonbury, you will pass the Abbot's Fish House at Meare, a medieval building used by the fisherman who kept the great abbey supplied with fish. In the surrounding field are depressions that were once fishponds, and Meare Pool, now dry land, once teemed with fish.

Glastonbury itself is rich in places to see, most with their accompanying legend. The church is a superb one in an area that is rich in fine churches. In the churchyard is one of the two thorn trees associated with the 'Holy Thorn' of Glastonbury. It is said that Joseph of Arimathea came to Britain to preach around AD 60. He leaned on his staff while praying, and it took root in the soil. It was claimed to flower every Christmas. The original tree was destroyed in Cromwell's time, but the one in the churchyard and that at the abbey are taken from cuttings.

The abbey is a majestic sight; the twin arches, sixty yards high, frame the ruin of a great abbey over two hundred yards long. At the Dissolution, the abbey was destroyed and the abbot killed, his head impaled on the abbey gate. The only building to survive virtually untouched was the Abbot's Kitchen. With four great fireplaces built into its corners, it is probably the finest example of a medieval kitchen anywhere in Europe. Like many other parts of the South West, Glastonbury is over-run with visitors in the summer months, both those coming to look at the ruins and those who hope to find inner peace in this land of legends. I suspect that both can be achieved with far less turmoil in the early spring or late autumn, when the crowds have disappeared.

From Glastonbury go north to Wells, with its magnificent cathedral, and then turn north-west to Cheddar, home of the eponymous cheese and of the magnificent Gorge. There are show caves there, too, but the Gorge is the greater natural wonder, and it has been spared the awful tweeness that mars the Cheddar caves and the more famous Wookey Hole near Wells.

From Cheddar take the road through Mendip Forest, crossing over the Mendip Hills to Compton Martin. In the village main street is the Ring o' Bells. The bar is sited in an opened-out old staircase, walked by a ghost at night. The same ghost also has a habit of opening the back door. A previous landlord stood milk bottles on the step to give himself warning of the ghost. The bottles remained on the step, but the next morning the back door was wide open once more.

The pub has a huge ingle-nook, at present unused, with a bread oven to one

The Ring o' Bells
Licensees: Richard & Jackie Owen
Compton Martin, Avon
☎ West Harptree (0761) 221284
11.30-2.30; 6.30 (7 in winter)-11

Butcombe Bitter; Marston Pedigree; Wadworth 6X

Lunchtime & evening food. Dining-room. Garden. Families welcome.

The Ring o' Bells, Compton Martin – beware of the ghost!

The unspoilt interior of the Tucker's Grave at Faulkland; the warm welcome soon makes you forget its grim past

side. There are flagged floors, wooden beams and table skittles in the bar, the lounge has a big open fire and there is a spacious dining-room looking out on to the gardens. Children can play on the slide outside and there is also a very well-appointed children's room, with table skittles and a rocking horse. Many pubs have children's rooms that are just one remove from padded cells; this one is a pleasure for both children and adults to use.

From Compton Martin head east, turning right in West Harptree towards Chewton Mendip, with the delicate stone tracery of its fine church tower. Follow the B roads towards Trowbridge and, after passing through the village of Faulkland, you will come to the Tucker's Grave Inn in a lonely spot a mile further on.

The pub would gladden the heart of Mabel Mudge, if she could see it. There are just two rooms, a 'best' room with an open fire and wooden settles, and a similar room, with wooden benches surrounding the central tables and the beer stillaged under the window sill. It is completely unaltered by the passage of time. Some tourists might sniffily dismiss it for its lack of 'facilities'; others will be delighted to find the friendly atmosphere of a pub with no pretensions, but a great deal of warmth.

The Tucker's Grave takes its name from a suicide, Edward Tucker, who hanged himself from the rafters of the barn in 1747, 'not having the fear of God before his eyes, but moved and seduced by the instigations of the

Tucker's Grave
Licensees: Mr & Mrs Swift
Faulkland, Somerset
☎ Faulkland (037 387) 230
11.30-2.30; 6-11

Draught Bass; Whitbread West Country Pale Ale; Cheddar Valley Cider

Food: ploughmans at lunchtime only. Garden. Camping.

Devil . . . came with force of armes . . . with a certain hempton cord value one peny which he the said Edward Tucker in both his hands then and there had and tied one end thereof to a Certain Beame in the said Barn and the other end about his neck did tie and with a corde so tied himself did feloniously and voluntarily choke and strangle with which such choking and strangling the said Edward Tucker then and there instantly died.'

You can read the original of this description in the Tucker's Grave and you are unlikely to be disturbed in your enjoyment of this unspoilt old-fashioned local by the shade of Edward Tucker.

Follow the same road a couple of miles further east and you come to Norton St Philip, home village of a completely different, but equally classic pub. The George was originally built to house merchants trading in wool and cloth with the nearby Hinton Priory, and is an imposing stone building, with a superb frontage. There is a massive oak door under the great stone porch, a flight of steps leading up to a tiny door to one side, half-timbering and mullioned windows. The main bar is traditionally furnished with settles and solid wooden tables; there is an oak-panelled lounge and a separate restaurant. Off the courtyard at the back is the Dungeon Bar, recalling that supporters of Monmouth were incarcerated there after the failure of his 'pitchfork' rebellion.

Monmouth and his motley army camped

The interior of the George at Norton St Philip. Supporters of Monmouth's rebellion were incarcerated in the dungeons below the inn

The George
Licensee: M. F. Moore
Norton St Philip, Somerset
☎ Faulkland (037 387) 224
10.30-2.30; 6-11

Draught Bass, Wadworth Devizes Bitter, 6X

Lunchtime & evening food. Restaurant. Families welcome. Courtyard.

overnight at Norton St Philip, and someone is alleged to have shot at him as he shaved in his room at the George. There was a skirmish, after which one of his generals had to amputate his own arm with one of the inn's carving-knives, and then Monmouth retreated to Sedgemoor, where he faced his final defeat.

The George is the last of our West Country classic pubs, but before sampling the delights of the Welsh ones, allow yourself the pleasure of a visit to Bath, one of the most beautiful Georgian cities in Europe. The spa waters, which gave the city

its fame, are tepid and fairly unpleasant tasting, but the great sweep of the Royal Crescent compensates for any amount of bad taste.

The city's roots go back into Celtic times, with the story of a prince, Bladud, banished because he had leprosy, who became a swineherd. He noticed that his pigs lost their skin diseases after wallowing in a muddy pool, tried the same thing himself and was cured. He returned home in triumph and later built a shrine at the site. The invading Romans were much taken with the waters of Bath as well, and the springs continued to be used in medieval times, though their greatest vogue came in the eighteenth century. 'Taking the waters' gained the seal of royal approval and fashionable society flocked to the spa towns, the greatest of which was Bath.

After enjoying the splendours of Bath, travel up past Bristol and across the Severn by the soaring road bridge into Wales.

The superb, half-timbered frontage of the George, Norton St Philip

To Wales and
the Welsh Borders

'When you see three lone Scots pines in the Welsh
landscape, generally where the bare hill country
reaches down to the cultivated valleys, there you
are likely to find some old farm or tavern where
the drovers used to spend their nights – blowing
their horns to announce their coming, corralling
their beasts in the Halfpenny Field behind, and
settling down themselves to ale and roistering.'

THE MATTER OF WALES
JAN MORRIS

Driving west or north in Wales you will increasingly hear the lilt of the Welsh language being spoken. There is a good deal of genteel paranoia amongst English people about the Welsh language. No dinner party conversation is complete without the anecdote about an English person going into a Welsh pub or shop where the people instantly change from talking in English to Welsh. In truth, Welsh people are much the same as people anywhere; show some respect for them, their culture and their country, and they will show some respect for you. The friendly welcome is as much a Welsh as an English prerogative.

One strange phenomenon, however, in a land not alleged to have too much fondness for things English, is that the sign for pubs called 'The Cross' always seems to be the cross of St George, the patron saint of England, rather than St David, the Welsh saint.

Though we English tend to regard the pub as our creation and our sole property, there are in Wales, in proportion to its size, just as many excellent pubs as in England, and certainly as many country classics. The first of them lies to the west of Cardiff, not far from the airport.

The landmarks that lead you to the Blue Anchor at East Aberthaw are an enormous cement works and a power station with a vast chimney belching smoke into the sky. If that sounds a strange adjunct to a classic country pub, the Blue Anchor is good enough to make you overlook its ugly giant of a neighbour.

Aberthaw is just East of Cardiff's Rhoose Airport, and the Blue Anchor lies just off the B4265. It is an old smuggler's inn, and the story goes that there are three tunnels running underground from it, one to the beach, one to the cottage across the road and one to the nearby castle. Under the thatched roof is a tangle of linked rooms: a stone-flagged, beamed bar with a large open fireplace, oak benches and a dartboard; another bar with gleaming brass and a plaque dating the pub to 1380; and a tiny room reached by a normal door or a very low archway. At the back is another room with an open fireplace and alongside it an old bread oven.

Sitting outside on the wooden benches, you can enjoy the flowers sprouting from barrels along the front wall and almost forget about the cement works and the power station. East Aberthaw is not the ideal place for sea bathing, but you can always walk down to the shore by a bridge over the railway and

Opposite: The Blue Anchor, East Aberthaw, a country oasis in an industrial desert

The Blue Anchor
Licensee: W. J. G. Coleman
East Aberthaw, South Glamorgan
☎ St Athan (0446) 750077
11.30-3.30; 5.30-11

Brain Dark, SA; Flowers IPA; Marston Pedigree; Robinson Best Bitter; Theakston Old Peculier; Wadworth 6X

Food at lunchtime (snacks only in the evening). Garden. Families welcome.

skim a few stones across the water instead.

When leaving East Aberthaw, turn left at the top of the road and follow the coast towards Bridgend. Pick up the A48 going west, turn off towards Porthcawl, then take the right turn that leads you to Kenfig. The Prince of Wales is on the right of the road, set high above the sand dunes which play such a major part in the history of Kenfig.

The Prince of Wales has been carefully restored; its stone walls once housed the Guildhall, and the upstairs room, reached from outside, still plays host to the parish council and to the weekly Sunday School. As you enter the pub, there is a small room to your left with a brick fireplace and an old high-backed settle. The main bar has a fine collection of polished brass and copper on the stone walls and a big blazing fire. There is also a small side room with a piano and another fireplace. The pub provides an excellent menu, including locally caught fish and sea-food, and Welsh delicacies such as laver bread (which is not bread, but sea-weed) and cawl (a lamb stew).

The Prince of Wales is all that remains of the ancient city of Kenfig, buried beneath the sand dunes running down to the sea. Among the ruins is said to be a church built by Morgan Mwyn Mawr, the founder of Glamorgan in AD 520. Eight hundred years ago the city was a thriving commercial centre, with a navigable river, a large seaport, and a castle

The Prince of Wales
Licensee: J. David
Kenfig, Mid Glamorgan
☎ Kenfig Hill (0656) 740356
11.30-4; 6-11

Draught Bass; Marston Pedigree; Sam Powell Best Bitter, Samson Strong Ale; Worthington Best Bitter

Lunchtime food, snacks such as pies and pasties in the evening. Families welcome. Garden.

The Prince of Wales looks out across the ancient buried city of Kenfig

surrounded by a moat forty-five feet wide and fifteen feet deep.

In 893, Kenfig suffered its first great disaster, when it was sacked and burned by the 'Black Pagans' (Vikings), and between then and 1402 it was put to the torch no fewer than eight times. A greater enemy even than the gangs of marauders, however, was the sand. The position was already serious in 1445, when Leland visited the area: 'There is a village on the East side of Kenfig and a castell, both in ruins and almost choked and devoured with the sandes that the Severn sea castith up.'

Great sandstorms were frequent, and eventually the city, with its hospital, law courts and church, was suffocated by the sand. The great storm of 1607 buried all traces of it, and it has remained hidden beneath the sands ever since.

From Kenfig you can see the industrial sprawl of Port Talbot and Swansea across the bay, and as you drive west, you have a bizarre contrast between the beautiful parkland and fine stately home of Margam Country Park on one side and the vast grimy spread of the Port Talbot steel-works on the other. Port Talbot is probably the last place you should think of stopping for a breath of Welsh air. High on a hill to your right, dead trees outlined against the sky show the effects of the smoke and pollution from the works. Lower down the slopes are more recent plantings that seem to be surviving; either the trees are hardier or the pollution less severe.

After Port Talbot things can only improve as you travel west. The landscape either side of Carmarthen is very much pocket handkerchief countryside: a tidy patchwork of small fields, hedges and woodland. In some ways it mirrors Devon, which faces it across the Bristol Channel. There are the same massive hedges as big as houses, but whereas the traditional roofing material in Devon is thatch, here in Wales it is, of course, Welsh slate.

Take the Tenby road west of Carmarthen, and then stay on the A477 until you see a turn to the north to Carew. The Carew Inn has an almost perfect setting. It is set on a hillside above an estuary that leads down past Pembroke to the sea. Across the road is a fine Celtic cross commemorating Maredudd ap Edwin, killed in battle in 1035, and beyond that is the eleventh-century Carew Castle. You can sit outside in the

garden at the front or in the yard at the back of the inn, and there is also a beer garden with swings and a slide. Inside is a small public bar and a homely lounge. The Carew Inn has a really friendly, cosy atmosphere and has been in the same family's ownership for fifty years.

As well as its castle, its Celtic cross and its excellent inn, Carew has one other unusual attraction, a tidal water mill, driven by the force of the sea rushing in past the mill at high tide and out again at low tide. The mill ceased operating about forty years ago and might have remained derelict from that day to this, but, eighteen years ago, people living nearby were woken during the night by a tremendous rumbling, crashing sound. They thought the mill must have collapsed, but when they got up the next morning they discovered that the blocks that had been put in to stop the wheels from turning years before had rotted and broken and the force of the tide had started the mill wheel turning again. It is still working today.

The whole of this part of Wales is studded with castles, and if you carry on north from Carew across the estuary and then take the road towards Haverfordwest, you will find another one. Turn north towards the lovely harbour town of Fishguard, with its houses clinging to the steep cliffs down to the sea. It is the departure point for ferries across to the Republic of Ireland, but our course takes us up the beautiful Pembrokeshire coast to what could easily be the next Welsh country classic, the Sailors' Safety at Dinas. Turn off the A487 in Dinas Cross and follow the sign to Pwll Gaelod. You drop down a narrow, steep, hedged lane into the isolated cove, and there stands the Sailors' Safety all alone, as it has since the sixteenth century.

If you are lucky, you may find the Sailors' Safety in rather more promising circumstances than I did on my visit. On a still, hot, late summer day, I took the road down to the cove, imagining a cool refreshing drink and a bite to eat, sitting outside in the sunshine, watching the waves lapping on the shore. As I turned the last bend, there was the pub, but my chances of refreshment of any sort were clearly nil – a bad fire had gutted it.

After, I hope, a more fruitful visit to Dinas than mine, travel on to the north. As you travel up the coast, for much of the way you can sense the sea as much as actually see it, catching only glimpses of it as a steep gorge or valley carves a gap

The Carew Inn
Carew, Dyfed
11-3; 5.30-11

Worthington Best Bitter

Lunchtime & evening snacks such as ploughmans or sandwiches. Garden. Families welcome.

The ruins of Carew Castle are a local landmark

Opposite: A Celtic cross stands sentinel over the Carew Inn

The Halfway Inn, halfway between Aberystwyth and Devil's Bridge. The beer flows almost as freely as the water of Wales

in the cliffs, but as you drop into Aberaeron, the sea is suddenly spread out before you, calm and deep blue on my last visit, on other days slate grey and white capped. The road runs for several miles along a ridge, with the sea to your left and to your right the Welsh Hills, growing steadily higher to the north towards Snowdonia. Just before you reach Aberystwyth, turn right on to the A4120 towards Devil's Bridge and drive up the valley high above the Afon (river) Rheidol for six miles to Pisgah, where you will find the Halfway Inn.

There are hundreds of similarly remote pubs scattered around the country. If they are to survive and prosper, their licensees have to work a little bit harder and be a bit more imaginative than those with a population on their doorsteps. On both counts, the owners of the Halfway Inn have been fully equal to the task; the inn has been sensitively restored to something approaching an original condition and it has a range of attractions that pull in customers from miles around.

The licensee, Keith Meese, is a man who believes that running a pub should be as much fun as going to one. You can be photographed 'imprisoned' in the stocks to one side of the door, inscribed with a motto from 1681: 'I am a sinner, I doth repent.' You can even serve yourself with beer from one of the many casks stillaged in the stone-walled bar. You still have to pay for the privilege, though your money has the good taste to disappear into a superb pre-decimal cash register. You can decipher the often barbed mottoes on the backs of the dining-room settles: 'Freely flows the water of Wales to England' is carved in Welsh on the back of one.

There are two bars, one with a stone fireplace, pine settles and benches and a dartboard, the other with slate-flagged floors, stone walls and the serve-yourself casks augmenting the beers dispensed from handpumps behind the bar. The range of beers available changes constantly, running through sixty-five variations at the last count. Outside there is a terrace above the inn from where you can enjoy the spectacular views down the valley towards the sea.

The food is excellent, the atmosphere friendly and the clientele pleasingly varied; you may find yourself talking to a local, a tourist or a student from the University at Aberystwyth. Families are made very welcome; you won't be made to feel like an outcast if you bring your children. In fact, there is only one thing wrong with the Halfway Inn: it is in one of the only two areas

The Halfway Inn
Licensee: Keith Meese
Pisgah, nr Aberystwyth, Dyfed
☎ Capel Bangor (097 084) 631
12-3; 6-11. Closed Sunday

Constantly changing range of beers

Lunchtime & evening food. Families welcome. Garden.

of mainland Great Britain that are still 'dry' on Sunday, so don't turn up hot and thirsty and dying for a drink then, because the pub is closed. The next referendum is in 1988; until then the Halfway Inn remains a weekday pleasure, not a Sunday treat.

The route to the next classic pub now lies east through the mountains, but you may wish to take a wander a little further up the coast before you resume the main purpose of the day. When you leave the Halfway Inn, travel back down the road to the first village, Pontycrug. At the end of the village, as the main road bears to the left, take the unsigned turn to the right. Follow the road as it drops steeply down, bear right across a railway line, cross the river and you are in the village of Capel Bangor. Turn left at the junction and then take the main road off to the right which leads you up to the lovely little town of Machynlleth, where Owain Glyndwr held a 'parliament' in 1404 and made his claim to be ruler of all Wales. Along the way you see the beginnings of the forests that are a feature of the drive north-west through the mountains, and, as you approach the town, you see the hills that lead up towards Snowdon rising beyond the town.

Just north of Machynlleth, you will find the Centre for Alternative Technology, devoted to finding ecologically acceptable, renewable sources of technology. It announces its presence from a hillside where several models of wind generators stand sentinel.

The half-timbered Horseshoe at Llanyblodwel is an old coaching inn on the banks of the Tanat

Between here and Dolgellau to the north you are in slate country. In the nineteenth century the quarries of Wales shipped out roofing slates to the whole of Britain and much of Europe as well. In its native land it was plentiful, widely available and cheap, and was used for virtually everything. Roofs, dry stone walls, fences, floors, and even manhole covers were made from it.

Beyond Dolgellau, make the brief journey north to Blaenau Ffestiniog, with its narrow-gauge railway running from the slate quarries high in the mountains to the sea. There are several nature reserves in the area and down on the coast you can choose from the contrasting attractions of Harlech Castle or Sir Clough Williams-Ellis's strange Italianate village, Portmeirion. Just to the north is Snowdon, highest mountain in Wales, reachable on foot or by the mountain railway.

When you are ready to resume the classic pub route, take the A494 north-east from Dolgellau. The road through the slatelands corkscrews its way between steep, thickly forested hillsides. Beyond Dolgellau it gradually becomes a gentler, more open road, with long straight stretches punctuated by sections which twist and turn and burrow beneath a canopy of trees. Finally, emerging from a wood, you see Bala Lake stretching away to the north-east ahead of you. On a sunny afternoon the lake is an inviting deep blue; on an overcast day it looks as cold and hard as slate. Bala Lake is hugely popular as a watersports area, and the surface is usually dotted with dinghies and sailboards.

At Bala village turn off to the south and follow the B roads up over the Berwyn Hills and down along the valley of the Tanat until you reach Llanyblodwel. The Horseshoe at Llanyblodwel sits by an old stone pack-horse bridge over the river. The bridge is so narrow that you are grateful for the 'refuges' in the sides of it, where you can look down the river without risk from any traffic on it.

The Horseshoe is a black-and-white half-timbered building. One or two of the walls look a little perilous, but the inn has stood there since the fifteenth century and will no doubt survive for a century or two yet. The beamed low-ceilinged bar is covered with china mugs, old glass bottles and key-rings, and there is a stone fireplace with seats recessed into it. The lounge contains a piano, which is drafted into use for weekend sing-songs, and there is a games room with a pool table.

The Horseshoe
Licensee: Phil Hindley
Llanyblodwel, Clwyd
☎ Llansantffraid (069 181) 227
11-2.30; 6 (7 in winter)-11

Marston Burton Bitter

Lunchtime & evening food. Outdoor drinking area. Accommodation.

Opposite: The three-storey 'tower' brewery at the Three Tuns, Bishops Castle

The road outside used to be the main road from Llangedwyn to Llansantffraid, and the Horseshoe was a coaching inn. Two horses were kept permanently stabled in the barn alongside the inn; they were hitched to each coach to help on the pull up the steep hill behind the Horseshoe, and then returned to await the next one.

There is no suggestion of a main road past the pub now; it is in a quiet corner of a quiet village, with a fine setting by the river. You can sit out at wooden tables by the riverbank, or you could stay for a night or two and try your luck at fly-fishing. The Horseshoe has rights to a mile-long stretch of the river.

Before you leave the village, wander down to the church. There has been a church on the site for centuries, but the present building dates largely from 1845 to 1860, when the incumbent parson, also an artist and an enthusiast of Gothic architecture, restored and rebuilt the church to his own designs and largely at his own expense. There is an unusual curved stone spire and much painted and decorated stonework inside.

The Three Tuns, Bishops Castle, survives passing fads and fashions by brewing its own, surprisingly potent, ale

At Llanyblodwel, you are very close to Offa's Dyke, the eighth-century earthwork which runs the length of the Welsh borders. Follow the line of it south on the road through Welshpool and Montgomery, where Offa's Dyke and the present Welsh border coincide. Owain Glyndwr tried and failed to take the castle; it stood until destroyed by Cromwell, and its ruins still dominate the town. From Montgomery, the B4385 will lead you to Bishops Castle.

Bishops Castle has no castle and no bishop. The former was cannibalised by the inhabitants of this close-knit community centuries ago and built into the fabric of the many Tudor and Stuart buildings that now adorn the border town.

The Three Tuns, like the Blue Anchor at Helston, is one of the tiny band of pubs which survived to the mid-1970s as a home brewery. It is the only one of that elite band to have its own 'tower' brewery, a three-storey arrangement by which the ingredients for the brew are fed into the top of the brewhouse. They are boiled, fermented and racked, emerging at the ground floor as finest ale.

There has been a pub on the site since 1640, but the current brewery building was constructed towards the end of the nineteenth century. The three-bar pub boasts a straightforward but attractive public bar, and a plusher but unassuming lounge. Both have wood-burning stoves. There is also a

The Three Tuns
Licensees: J. & D. Wood
Bishops Castle, Shropshire
☎ Bishops Castle (0588) 638797
11.30-2.30; 6.30-11

John Roberts Mild, XXX, Castle Steamer, Old Scrooge (winter brew)

Bar snacks lunchtime & evening. Families welcome, but limited accommodation. Courtyard drinking area.

small side bar where families can be accommodated.

The principal attractions of the place are its ales, named after the Roberts family who ran the pub for five generations, and the ales are well worth a long journey. The pale, deceptively innocent-looking bitter is the best-known brew, but there is also a distinctive, characterful mild and the dark, malty Castle Steamer.

The pub is typical of the best in border inns, its atmosphere matching that of the town. An autumn evening will find the surrounding area heavy with the scent of woodsmoke, silent as the mountains that roll from beyond its western edge. Give the Wood family a week's notice out of season, and they will be happy to show you round the brewery.

O ur next classic pub is also a home-brew pub; of the modern era, but with an unashamedly old-fashioned atmosphere. From Bishops Castle take the B4385 towards Craven Arms, one of the dozen Shropshire towns deriving its name from that of the roadside inn around which it grew. Just south of Craven, take time to visit Stokesay Castle, a moated manor house from the thirteenth century, which has survived in remarkably good condition. Little imagination is required to see how it would have functioned in its heyday.

Better known is the ancient town of Ludlow, now thankfully by-passed by the A49. One of the saddest sights is the interior of the Feathers Hotel, the world-famous half-timbered inn at the centre of the town. A single lounge bar replaced the many-roomed drinking area years ago, and as yet there are no plans to make the interior match the spectacular external appearance.

Take the A4117 Bewdley road out of Ludlow and climb Clee Hill to experience a sudden change in scenery, the craggy landscape resembling moorland for a time, before descending to picturesque Cleobury Mortimer, with its half-timbered buildings and permanent flood of day-trippers. Immediately beyond Cleobury, turn left towards Kinlet and trust that you spot the signs to Stottesdon.

Stottesdon, far from the madding crowd, yet only forty minutes from the West Midlands conurbation, is many people's vision of 'Ambridge': a quiet backwater, full of characters, and displaying no outward signs of recognising the existence of the twentieth century. 'Dasher' Downing's pub, the Fox & Hounds, is charmingly disorganised, and long may it remain so. In the smarter bar you may

The Fox & Hounds, Stottesdon, 'Dasher' Downing's idiosyncratic, but excellent, pub

The Fox & Hounds
Licensee: Malcolm Downing
Stottesdon, Shropshire
12-2.30; 7-11 (Closed Monday lunchtime)

Downings DDD (Dasher Downing's Draught), Superdash; Guest beers

Bar snacks in the evenings only. A skittle alley may be booked by prior arrangement.

notice that none of the furnishings matches any other. It hardly matters. There may be the odd dog or two curled up on the seats round the fire and you will be lucky to shift them; they have been there longer than you, after all. The public bar is more basic; it has fewer chairs.

'Dasher' gets the odd special beer in when the mood takes him; he likes the variety. It rarely matches the pub's own beer, though, brewed out at the back in what must be one of the smallest brewhouses in the world. You cannot tour the brewery, but if you shine a torch through the window, you will see most of it.

A few years back 'Dasher' was prosecuted for serving after time. He told the magistrates that the law was an ass, but it did not have much effect. His locals drew a cartoon of the raid, showing the police leaping through the pub windows, while a mugging went on in the background, unattended. Such excitements are unlikely to attend your visit, but if pubs are about relaxation, this one is a gem; no muzak, no machines and an impression of timelessness.

The most picturesque route to our next classic pub will take you through some of the most beautiful and little-known countryside of the West Midlands. Take the road back to Cleobury Mortimer, turning left towards Bewdley, then take the right turn to Abberley, the first village to appear in the 'Domesday Book'. Note the ghostly tower, bats and all, that rises from Abberley School. At Great Witley, take the Bromyard Road across the Abberley Hills, past Upper Sapey and Tedstone Wafre, then over the sheep-scattered downs above Bromyard town. The cathedral city of Hereford is worth a stop, and in the summer traffic it may be compulsory. Take the opportunity to visit the Museum of Cider, if you wish, next to Bulmer's massive works.

Travelling on the A49 from Hereford to Ross-on-Wye, take the left turn to Hoarwithy and from there follow the signs to Carey. The area around Hereford is so awash with excellent pubs that, as in the Bermuda triangle, there is a great danger of the unwary traveller disappearing, never to be seen again. If such is your fate, you could do worse than make your disappearance at the delightful Cottage of Content at Carey. You approach it down a 'hollow way' so deep and steep that it looks like an overgrown tunnel. Emerging into the daylight again, you'll find the pub sitting beyond a little bridge, sheltered by a vast

The Cottage of Content
Licensee: Peter Nash
Carey, Hereford & Worcester
☎ Carey (043 270) 242
11.30-2.30; 6.30-11

Hook Norton Best Bitter, Old Hookey; Guest beers

Lunchtime & evening food. Accommodation. Garden. Families welcome.

Opposite: The Cottage of Content at Carey. Was ever a pub better named?

horse-chestnut tree. 'Straight off the lid of a 1930s biscuit tin' was one description given to me, and certainly there are times when it looks almost too good to be true – especially just before opening time on a hot summer afternoon!

There is a garden and terrace behind the inn, but even better, take your drink out to the flower-covered front terrace or sit on the wooden bench under the chestnut tree and listen to the stream slipping by. If there is more than one car passing every half-hour, it is a busy day.

The inn is over five hundred years old and its interior seems little changed by the centuries: a warren of small, homely oak-beamed rooms with plain, comfortable furniture. The food is mostly home-made and very good value, and you can stay the night in the simple, comfortable bedrooms, secure in the knowledge that your sleep is unlikely to be disturbed. If ever a pub was well named, the Cottage of Content is the one.

After leaving Carey, probably well contented, travel down through Ross-on-Wye, a pretty town in a beautiful wooded setting above the river, and follow the Wye down to Monmouth. It stands guard where the Wye merges with the Monnow, a strategic point whose importance was recognised by the Romans. The eleventh-century castle was the birthplace of Henry V, the medieval fortified gateway on the bridge over the Monnow is unique in Britain.

South of Monmouth you could follow the Wye to the beautiful, delicate remains of Tintern Abbey, but our route now lies to the north. Follow the B4347 that runs alongside the River Monnow, crossing the main A465 road from Abergavenny to Hereford, from Ewyas Harold follow the signs for Dulas. The Trout Inn is on a bend in the little-used road a mile or so beyond Dulas. If you are tall, watch out as you enter the pub; not all headaches are beer-induced!

The Trout also carries the nickname the 'Found Out', and there are two schools of thought on the origins of the name. The more prosaic explanation is that it is so called simply because it is so hard to find. This has some ring of truth. On my first visit I stopped to ask the way from the driver of a car going in the opposite direction, who said that she had heard of it, but could not place it. When I rounded the next bend in the road, the 'Found Out' was right in front of me. More interesting, if less plausible, is the tale told by a few locals who claim that the nickname

The Trout Inn ('The Found Out')
Dulas, nr Ewyas Harold, Gwent
☎ Golden Valley (0981) 240356
11-2.30; 6-11

Hereford Bitter; Wood Special Bitter; Bulmers Traditional Draught Cider

Food: sandwiches and ploughmans only, though meals are provided to order. Garden. Families welcome.

The Trout Inn ('The Found Out') at Dulas. Hard to find but, with its peaceful setting, harder still to leave

arose from the case of a local farmer who was caught in *flagrante delicto* with someone else's wife; he was found out and the name stuck.

Whichever explanation you prefer, you will be delighted to discover the pub; it is that much over-worked cliché, 'a gem'. There is a garden with a stream at the back and a little terrace at the front, where you can sit and relax over a leisurely pint with no sound louder than the birdsong or the bleating of a sheep to disturb you. On summer Saturdays you can watch the pub cricket team in action on the field across the road that they share with the licensee's sheep and goats.

Inside you will find an absolutely delightful pub; a bar full of antiques, bric-à-brac and traditional pub games like skittles and quoits, a lounge with well-worn, but very comfortable armchairs. If you can't relax at the 'Found Out', you can't relax at all. There is good beer from local breweries and there are no space invaders, piped muzak or other delights of the electronic age.

The 'Found Out' is the sort of pub that makes you wish there were no such things as closing time, work or Monday mornings, but if you can summon the will-power to move on, you will arrive at what must be the most beautifully sited pub in Britain.

Retrace your steps to the A465 and turn north at Crucorney, five miles north of Abergavenny. Or, more adventurously, head across country, skirting the back of Pandy before plunging into the rising valley of Afon Honddu, with the wall of the Black Mountains rising to the west. Five miles north, beyond Stanton and Cwmyoy, the road will lead you to the Priory and the Abbey Hotel at Llanthony.

It is claimed that in the sixth century the patron saint of Wales, Saint David, built a wattle and daub cell on the site of the parish church which bears his name. Though this fell into ruin over the succeeding centuries, a Norman Priory (which is what it was, despite the name of the hotel) was established on the site in 1108; the magnificent remains visible today date from about one hundred years later. The activities of Welsh brigands sweeping down from the mountains were a constant problem to the Priory, and even before Henry VIII's Dissolution of the Monasteries, it had lost most of its importance, and its revenues. In the eighteenth century it found secular use as a shooting lodge before becoming a hotel.

The Abbey Hotel has a single stone-flagged and stone-arched bar, originally the undercroft of the prior's and canons' quarters. There is a lovely dining-room with a curved oak high-backed settle and much old china and gleaming brass. You can spend the night in a four-poster bed in one of the rooms in the tower, though the stone spiral staircase is not recommended to those of a nervous disposition or those who have drunk too deeply of the beer dispensed straight from the casks stillaged behind the bar.

There are benches outside, facing across lawns studded with the ruined arches of the Priory. Beyond is the dark mass of the Black Mountains. It would be hard to imagine a more beautiful place to stay the night; for that reason you will have to book well in advance if you hope to do so.

I f you can tear yourself away from the Priory and, if your nerves can stand the excitement, take the single-track road that leads north from Llanthony. After a few miles and perhaps a few near misses, you will emerge above the tree-line and will be rewarded for your bravery by a stunning panorama of the Wye Valley far below you. Drink your fill of the view, then head down into Hay-on-Wye to drink your fill in the Blue Boar, on the right-hand side of the B4350 as you enter Hay from the west.

Hay is the world capital of the second-hand book trade. Every other shop sells books, and they are sold in converted churches, mills, schools, warehouses and just about every other kind of building as well; they may even be sold in converted pubs for

Opposite: The graceful stone arches of the ruined Priory frame the Abbey Hotel at Llanthony

The Abbey Hotel
Licensee: Ivor Prentice
Llanthony, Gwent
☎ Crucorney (087 32) 487
11-3; 6-11

Brain Bitter; Flowers IPA, Original; Ruddle County

Restaurant Tuesday to Friday evenings. Bar meals lunchtimes and Saturday to Monday evenings. Garden. Families welcome. Accommodation. The hotel is closed from mid-December to Easter.

The Blue Boar
Licensees: John & Lucy Golesworthy
Castle Street, Hay-on-Wye, Hereford & Worcester
☎ Hay-on-Wye (0497) 820884
11-2.30; 6-11

EST.ᴰ 1742

Flowers IPA, Original; Bulmers Traditional Cider

Food lunchtimes only. Families welcome.

all I know, though that would be taking things a bit too far. A shop across the road from the Blue Boar sells books by weight, £1.50 a kilogram, a development that must have sensitive bibliophiles tearing their first folios out by the roots.

Have a browse through the accumulated verbiage of the centuries, find yourself a good book, then settle down in a corner of the Blue Boar for a quiet hour or so. It is an auction room cum town hall cum the best pub in town; lots of bustle, lots of life, but with plenty of room for those who just want a quiet chat or to sit in silence, immersing themselves in the dusty world of some long-forgotten

The windows of the Blue Boar look out on Hay-on-Wye, a bibliophile's dream town

writer. The beer is good and the lunches are excellent. Linger a while, but not too long: the next classic pub is an absolute beauty.

Those with no romance in their souls will now head for Whitney-on-Wye by leaving Hay to the north-east and taking the main road to the Rhydspence Inn, just off the A438 one mile west of Whitney. Romantics with thirty pence to spend will prefer to take the direct route which crosses one of Britain's few remaining privately owned toll-bridges. You can stop at the tollhouse to buy a history of the bridge or for a cup of tea, which you can drink watching the Wye drift by, but if you are there during licensing hours, you are wasting valuable drinking time that could be spent in the Rhydspence Inn.

The Rhydspence is an ancient half-timbered mule-drovers' inn that would be on many people's shortlist for the best pub in Britain. There is a massive entrance porch, and inside you will find an oak-beamed bar with a big stone fireplace and gleaming copper and brass. Leading off it is the smaller locals' bar, full of character and characters. You can play table quoits, dominoes and darts, drink good beer and eat superb meals either in the bar or the dining-room. There are fine views of the Wye Valley from the inn itself and from its terraces and lovely sloping gardens, complete with resident ducks on a small stream.

The Rhydspence is just in England, though if you turn left as you leave the pub,

The Rhydspence Inn at Whitney-on-Wye, a magnificent, half-timbered thirteenth-century inn

The Rhydspence Inn
Licensee: Peter Glover
Whitney-on-Wye,
Hereford & Worcester
☎ Clifford (049 73) 262
11-2.30; 7-11

Hook Norton Best Bitter;
Robinson Best Bitter;
Dunkertons Cider

Lunchtime & evening food. Restaurant. Accommodation. Garden. Families welcome.

you will be in Wales before you can say 'Powys'. Why the English and Welsh used to fight all the time, with a place like this on their borders where they could have settled their differences over a friendly pint and a game of darts, will remain forever a mystery.

The route now lies north towards the far-distant Lake District, but on the way there is one last Welsh classic pub to visit, in perhaps the most beautiful riverside setting imaginable. To reach it, you must follow the Welsh border almost as far as Wrexham. Go north through Oswestry and take the A5 past the thirteenth-century Chirk Castle. Take the Wrexham road, crossing over the Llangollen Canal, and at Ruabon turn east on to the A539. Follow the road until you reach the village of Erbistock.

A sign to the right directs you towards

the Boat Inn, and you follow it down a series of winding country lanes as you drop towards the River Dee. At the bottom of the last, steep hill you will come to a pleasant hamlet, where there is a fine church and, just beyond it, a pub with an unrivalled view across the river.

The Boat at Erbistock sits on a bend of the Dee, with beautiful vistas of the river in both directions. The immaculate flowerbeds are a riot of colour, and there are lawns sloping down to the water's edge. A ferry boat once plied the river here, and the landing-stage and the windlass used to draw it to and fro are still in position.

The Boat Inn at Erbistock looks out on the River Dee, one of Britain's great salmon rivers

The Boat Inn is actually two buildings. One, the River Room, serves good bar food; the other contains an excellent restaurant and a bar which is a complement to the setting the pub occupies: stone flags, oak beams, polished brass, a vast fireplace and old oak chairs and settles.

The Boat is such an outstanding pub in such a wonderful position, that it is not surprisingly overwhelmed with people on summer weekends. If you chance upon it on a fine day in early spring or in autumn, you can enjoy its peace and its beauty relatively alone, sitting at the tables on the gravel terraces or on the lawns, watching the river drift by below you. This is the last Welsh pub we shall visit on this journey through Wales and the Welsh borders; there could scarcely be a better one to remember Wales by.

The Boat Inn
Licensee: Mrs H. G. Mostyn
Erbistock, Clwyd
☎ Bangor-on-Dee (0978) 780143
11-2.30; 6-11

Tetley Bitter

Lunchtime & evening food. Restaurant. Garden. Families welcome.

To the Lake District

'I have taken a long solitary ramble to-day. These
gigantic mountains piled on each other, these
waterfalls, these million-shaped clouds tinted by
the varying colours of innumerable rainbows
hanging between yourself and a lake as smooth
and dark as a plain of polished jet – oh, these are
sights attainable to the contemplation.'

'LETTER TO MISS HITCHENER'
SHELLEY

A wooden plaque in the Dusty Miller at Wrenbury. Despite its long and varied history, it has been a pub for less than ten years

We left Wales at a waterside pub, and now we re-enter England to visit another one, this time at the side of a canal. The Llangollen Canal, a sideshoot of the Shropshire Union Canal, is one of the most popular and most beautiful stretches of inland waterway in Britain. There are two superb aqueducts on the canal and some fine country to travel through; there is also an excellent pub which makes a fine place to begin and end a journey on the waterways.

The Dusty Miller at Wrenbury is a pub with a history that is even more chequered than usual in pubs. As its name suggests, it was originally a working mill, dating back to the sixteenth century, with an underpass wheel straddling the infant River Weaver which you cross by a footbridge from the car-park.

At the beginning of this century, it ceased to function as a mill and became a warehouse and collection point for locally grown fruit and vegetables, which were transported to the hungry city of Manchester in 'fly boats', taking two days to make the journey. After the war, the building began to decay, but it was rescued from dereliction by the present owners in 1977. They opened it as a pub, with an upstairs restaurant and private bar.

From the bar, you can watch the traffic on the canal outside and the functioning of the canal bridge, which is operated by a counterpoise weight, and is claimed to have

The Dusty Miller
Licensees: Mr & Mrs Lloyd-Jones
Wrenbury, nr Nantwich, Cheshire
☎ Nantwich (0270) 780537
11-2.30; 6-11

Robinson Best Mild, Best Bitter

Lunchtime & evening food. Restaurant (summer evenings and by appointment at other times). Garden. Families welcome.

been designed by Thomas Telford. You can also sit outside, among the rose gardens on the canal bank, and on fine summer days there are barbecues on the terrace.

We have already seen how often the village pub and the village church sit side by side, the twin pillars of English life for centuries. The next two classic pubs are both particularly fine examples of this co-existence; lovely villages, fine churches and superb pubs.

Drive north-east from Wrenbury, through the rich Cheshire grazing land and the town of Nantwich, a collection of half-timbered buildings listing at crazy angles, but still surviving the centuries. Pass Crewe, the home of Rolls-Royce motor cars and a station that has witnessed more human misery from passengers waiting in vain for connecting trains than probably any other in Britain.

After Crewe, take the Congleton road and, at the end of a sharp bend, turn left to Somerford Booths. Carry on straight over the main road and a little way on you will pick up a sign to Swettenham. Follow the road as it winds through farm and woodland and, after you cross the River Dane, take the left turn. You pass Swettenham Hall and then turn off to the left again into Swettenham village, a sleepy collection of houses with a church built of stone and old brick. Behind the church is the Swettenham Arms.

The rambling old building has weavers' windows and three different rooflines; it looks

Inside the Swettenham Arms: once a nunnery, now reputed to be haunted by a nun's ghost

The Swettenham Arms
Licensee: Paula Brooks
Swettenham, Cheshire
☎ Lower Withington
(0477) 71284
11-2.30; 5.30-10.30 (11 Friday & Saturday). Supper licence in restaurant

Webster Green Label Best, Yorkshire Bitter, Samuel Webster's Choice; Wilsons Original Mild, Bitter

Lunchtime & evening food. Garden. Families welcome. Accommodation.

out to the churchyard across a wide forecourt surrounded by a thirty foot hedge of conifers. There are window-boxes full of flowers, roses growing up the front of the pub and a lawned garden to one side, set with wooden benches and tables. Inside are comfortable bars, and a restaurant. On Sunday there is a traditional roast lunch.

The Swettenham Arms has an eccentric history. It was once a nunnery. People coming from far away for funerals would stay overnight at the nunnery, and the ghostly figure of a nun is alleged to walk in the rectory and its gardens at night. Bodies were also stored in the pub overnight before burial in the churchyard, with the coffins being taken to the church by an underground passage leading from the pub.

Finding Swettenham may be a bit of an adventure. On my visit the landlord reported that twenty-two of the road signs in the area were missing; you either need an excellent sense of direction, a lot of luck, or some action from the local council to replace them.

The Warren de Tabley arms, sign of the Bells of Peover Opposite: Peover's beautiful church, and beyond, its excellent pub

L eave Swettenham by the same road, but turn left at the very sharp bend at the junction. Keep to the left until you reach the main road, then immediately take the Goostrey road. Through the trees on your right, you will see the enormous white dish of Jodrell Bank radio telescope looming up. Cross over the railway line and it is clearly visible looking down the tracks. Follow signs to Allostock and Lach Denis until you cross over the top of the M6, then turn right on to the B5081 which leads to the village of Peover. Take the right turn signed to the church and drive down the cobbled lane, turn left immediately before the church and you will find yourself in the yard of our next pub, the Bells of Peover.

The yard is surrounded by lawned gardens, one with rustic trellises and seats. There is a small pond in the middle of it, and there is a path to follow which takes you under a line of horse-chestnut trees. The coat of arms on the pub sign are the Warren de Tabley arms and the sign board is original, dating from 1839, and repainted roughly every forty years since then.

You can sit outside the front of the pub on wooden benches, or you can walk into the churchyard and look at the stunningly beautiful fourteenth-century stone and half-timbered church. The porch leading into the pub is smothered under a living arch of foliage. The dining-room is set with white linen, cut glass and fresh flowers on every

The Bells of Peover
Licensee: J. G. Fisher
Lower Peover, nr Knutsford, Cheshire
☎ Lower Peover (056 581) 2480
11-3; 5.30-11

Greenall Whitley Original Mild, Bitter

Lunchtime & evening food. Families welcome. Garden.

table. The bar is beautifully furnished with a fine old dresser covered with pewter plates, an open fire, wooden settles, and a long-case clock. The only occasional interruption to the peace and quiet of this beautiful setting is the noise of a jet high overhead on its way to and from Manchester's Ringway airport.

Coming out of the cobbled lane from the Bells of Peover, turn right and, just as you leave the village, take the left turn to Plumley. Keep straight on through Plumley and turn right at the junction with the main road, which will take you to the M6 or straight into Manchester.

The stone walls around the Ram's Head at Denshaw defy the worst of the Pennine weather

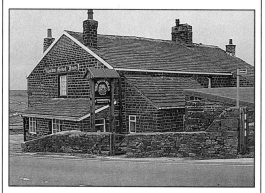

After the beauty and tranquillity of Lower Peover, our next classic pub is a rough, uncompromising-looking place in a bleak, windswept setting. It sits on the edge of the moors that separate Yorkshire from Lancashire and is best reached by avoiding Manchester altogether and sweeping round the city on the motorways that enclose it on three sides. If you want to see the capital of the area where cotton was once king, however, spend some time around the fringes of the city centre, where the city fathers have allowed a few of Manchester's fine Victorian buildings to remain untouched; then take the road east to Ashton-under-Lyne.

Follow the road towards Huddersfield as it climbs up into the foothills of the Pennines, with stone terraces of houses clinging to the steep hillsides. In some areas, the hillsides are so steep that houses are built on top of each other instead of back to back; the house will have four storeys on the lower side, with its bottom two storeys as one house on the lower street, and the upper two as a separate house opening on to the street above.

The towns and villages you pass through were once all mill-towns, now most of the mills are silent. The road runs parallel to the canal and railway line that tunnel through the Pennines. Now closed, the canal was once busy with traffic. Before the narrowboats were powered by engines, a horse would drag them to the mouth of the canal tunnel. Then the horse would be unhitched, for there was no tow-path in the tunnel, and the bargee would 'walk' the boat through the Pennines, by lying on his back and pushing against the roof of the tunnel with his feet.

None of the towns or villages you pass through could be described as pretty, it is not a word that sits easily on their solid stone walls; but they have a character and a strength that fits them perfectly to their landscape and their climate. Many of the houses have 'weavers' windows', a series of stone-mullioned windows across almost the full width of the house to admit the maximum amount of light for the weaving. In the days when all cloth manufacture was done by outworkers, weaving was done in virtually every home. You will often find terraces where the loft was open and continuous right along the row, with the weavers working on the top floor and living on the floors below.

After passing the impressive small town of Saddleworth and under a fine stone viaduct, turn left towards Dobcross and Delph. Turn right at the crossroads and keep straight on up towards the moors until you reach the Horse & Jockey on your left.

The Horse & Jockey is regularly battered by wild moorland weather, and its exterior betrays some evidence of the rough treatment it receives. Do not be put off the pub by its uncompromising exterior, however; its peeling paint conceals a homely and welcoming interior. The Kershaws have run the pub for some 28 years and you feel more like guests in their front room than paying customers. There is a snug room with leather seats and a comfy old sofa around an open fire and a bar with oak settles and panelled walls.

The Horse & Jockey is an old-fashioned pub. There is no food, no electronic games, no children's room, and the landlord keeps a few sheep to augment his living from the pub. It is a no-nonsense local pub, with no airs and graces but a welcome as straightforward and friendly as the people who live on these northern hills.

The next port of call is a pub in the same mould and not too far away. Drop back down the hill and fork off to the right at the sign to Delph. Turn right in the centre of the village and follow the A672 as it climbs up out of the village towards Halifax and the M62 motorway. At 1,200 feet above sea level, a couple of miles before you

Horse & Jockey
Licensee: David Kershaw
Stanedge, Delph, Greater Manchester
☎ Saddleworth (045 77) 4283
Open evenings 7-11; Saturday lunchtime only 1-3

Marston Owd Rodger; Moorhouse Pendle Witches Brew, Theakston Mild, Best Bitter, Old Peculier; Ward Bitter

No food. Families welcome at lunchtime. Camping available.

reach the motorway, you will find the Ram's Head, also known as 'Owd Tups', on your left.

Inside are three comfortable, characterful rooms, each with a roaring open fire on cold winter nights. You sit on carved oak settles or benches built into the part-panelled walls, and your beer may be pulled through a handpump or dispensed by gravity into jugs. Like the Horse & Jockey, it has restricted opening times: the only lunchtime you will find it open is Sunday, but visit on an evening or Sunday lunchtime and you will be captivated by its unspoilt and warmly welcoming atmosphere. If the weather is fair, take a walk

The beer at the Ram's Head at Denshaw is dispensed straight from the barrel into enamel jugs
Opposite: The sign of the Inn at Whitewell, a pub situated in the beautiful, but little-known, Forest of Bowland

The Ram's Head
Licensee: Geoffrey Haigh
Ripponden Road, Denshaw, Greater Manchester
☎ Saddleworth (045 77) 4802

Open evenings 6.30-11; Sunday lunchtime only

Theakston Dark Mild, XB, Best Bitter, Old Peculier

over the surrounding moors; if it is wild, watch the rain lash against the windows from the comfort of an inn that has provided a welcome refuge for travellers for centuries.

As you leave Denshaw, carry on up to the motorway and turn west, passing under a graceful, soaring arch which carries the Pennine Way. For once I would travel on the motorway unless you have a particular desire to see the declining cotton towns to the north of Manchester. Travel west along the M62 and M61 and after joining the M6 turn off to the east at the junction with the A59 just outside Preston. After a few miles, turn left on to the B6245. The road drops down into the Ribble valley, crossing the river over a stone bridge by a pub called the De Tabley Arms, a coat of arms we also encountered at the Bells of Peover. In the middle of the Roman town of Ribchester, turn right, following the Roman road north to the summit of Longridge Fell, where there is a fine view out over the Forest of Bowland. Drop down the other side, following the signs to Whitewell.

Though the Forest of Bowland does contain a lot of woodland, the word 'forest' has been used in the Norman sense, meaning an area of land reserved for the King's hunting. A vast amount of England was used for this purpose under the Normans, and the penalties for taking the King's game, or even for disturbing the ground by prospecting for minerals, were very severe. The pub we are now heading towards was once the chief keeper's house in the deer park in the royal forest of Bowland.

The Forest of Bowland is far less well known than the Lake District or the Yorkshire Dales. Outside the North it has scarcely been heard of at all, but it is an area of great beauty and variety, with narrow, thickly wooded river valleys, rolling pastures and open heather moorland. As you near Whitewell, the road bends and twists through beech woods, dropping towards the River Hodder. As you reach the floor of the valley, you find the village of Whitewell, with its inn and church, set above the river in a beautiful woodland setting.

T he Inn at Whitewell was originally a manor house, where the keeper of the King's deer park lived in the fourteenth century. Alongside it was a chapel, now the church of St Michael, where travellers would pause to pray for their safety, before travelling on down to Lancaster through the outlaw-infested hills to the north west. The inn belonged to the Towneley family in the nineteenth century, and it is claimed that they bought it as a result of a trick.

When the inn was to be auctioned, Lord Towneley had let it be known that he would be attending to buy it, and the sale was delayed pending his much overdue arrival. In the meantime a very loud, very drunk and very irritating tramp in the front row of the auction room kept up a barrage of demands that the place be sold, with or without Lord Towneley. To fill in the time while awaiting his arrival, the auctioneer held a mock sale, and, as a joke, knocked the property down to the tramp for a bargain price. The tramp instantly sobered up, revealed himself as Lord Towneley, and enforced the contract of sale that the auctioneer had just made.

The inn is a whitewashed, stone-

The transport at the Inn at Whitewell takes you back in time

The Inn at Whitewell
Licensee: Richard Bowman
Whitewell, Forest of Bowland, Clitheroe, Lancashire
☎ Dunsop Bridge (020 08) 222
11-3; 6-11. Open all day for teas & coffees

Moorhouse's Premium Bitter, Pendle Witches Brew

Lunchtime & evening food. Accommodation. Families welcome. Garden.

mullioned building, with Georgian and Victorian extensions. It belongs to the Queen as part of the Duchy of Lancaster and still retains its associations with field sports. Grouse and pheasant shooting can be arranged in season, and the inn has the fishing rights to five miles of both banks of the river, where you can fish for salmon and trout.

You will often find fish on the menu, including local smoked salmon, and game in season, black pudding 'to the apple' and a foot-long Cumberland sausage as well. There is probably the biggest and best wine list of any pub in the country, for the owners are also wine-shippers. You can even buy the inn's own brand of locally made, top-quality shirts, shooting stockings, for which they have royal customers, and hand-lasted shoes. There is also an art gallery, where you can buy paintings by artists from all over Britain.

There are carved stone fireplaces, oak beams, wood-panelling, oak settles, a long-case clock and even a baby grand piano in the corner of the lounge, with a resident pianist on Wednesday and Saturday. It remains very definitely a pub, not just a hotel, and to prove it there is a taproom as well, the Hodder Bar, with a pool table. In fine weather, you can sit outside at wooden tables high above the river and enjoy the peace and beauty of the country and the comfort and atmosphere of a classic country pub. The Inn at Whitewell makes a fine place to spend a few days, whether you are interested in shooting and fishing or just want to spend some time walking in the woods, valleys and moors of the Forest of Bowland.

From Whitewell take the road north towards Dunsop Bridge, then follow the road to Lancaster. You climb through steep, bracken-covered hillsides and emerge into steadily more open countryside. At last, without any advance warning, you find yourself high on a ridge with a panoramic view of Lancaster, Morecambe Bay and the South Cumbrian coast. You will see the Heysham nuclear power station on the Lune estuary, and our route takes us close, but not too close to it.

You descend into Lancaster past the observatory set on a hilltop in Williamson Park. Pass through the handsome city and leave on the road towards Morecambe and Heysham, which gives you excellent views of the cathedral and castle as you cross the Lune. Turn left on to the B5273 to Middleton and Overton, and then go left again, following

**The Golden Ball
(Snatchems)**
Licensees: Fred & Lesley Jackson
Snatchems, Overton,
nr Lancaster, Lancashire
☎ Lancaster (0524) 63317
10.45-3; 6-11

Mitchell Mild, Bitter, ESB

Bar snacks (sandwiches and pies) lunchtime & evening. Families welcome. Garden.

the sign to the same places. You will also see a sign warning you that there is no through road at high tide.

A short distance along, perched above the road beyond the reach of the tidal waters, is the Golden Ball. The wall alongside the pub is covered with brambles and dog roses, and you can sit out in the garden at the back or at tables on the terrace at the front, looking back across Lancaster as the tide flows in and out. At high tide the road is completely submerged, so you may have the awful experience of being trapped in a pub until the tide goes out again! The high water mark is so high that the spring tides lap at the doorstep.

The Golden Ball, also known as 'Snatchems', has a walled garden at the back for warm days

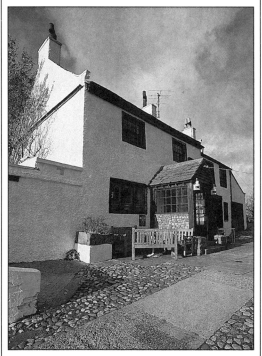

The Golden Ball is a tiny, very homely local with open fires burning in the cosy, low-beamed rooms. There is a parlour with oak benches set into the walls, and a low doorway leads to a snug with a fine carved chair and a serving hatch. The end bar is a marvellously warm and comfortable place to sit out the ebb and flow of the tides.

The origins of the name 'Snatchems' are inevitably the subject of some dispute, with three rival versions vying for acceptance. One is that it is named because crews of ships on their way down the Lune used to send in a rowing boat so that they could snatch a few drinks; another is that the inflowing Lune on the high tide was so full of salmon that you could lean over the wall and snatch them; but the most plausible is that it comes from the times when the press-gang would collect unwilling recruits for the Royal Navy, by descending on the pub and snatching those too drunk to make their escape.

On leaving Snatchems, either retrace your steps into Lancaster and take the A6 or the M6 north towards the Lake District, or have a look at the genteel resort of Morecambe before heading north round the coast.

The chances of wandering as lonely as a cloud in the Lake District are still surprisingly good. The area contains some of England's most spectacular landscapes and is tremendously popular as a holiday destination as a result, but it is still possible to get right away from the crowds that throng

The interior of the Masons Arms, Strawberry Bank. Perhaps the best pub in the Lake District; wonderful food and a bewildering range of beers from all over the world

Ambleside and Windermere and find places where your only companion is your own shadow.

The Lakes attract everyone from mountaineers and hikers to people who simply want to meander round in their cars admiring the view, and the Lake District pubs reflect these differences. Some are brash and basic boozers, others are lavishly appointed hotels; I've chosen a selection that covers the whole range; each, in its different way, is a classic.

The first, and maybe the best, of the Lakeland classics is the Masons Arms at Strawberry Bank on Cartmel Fell. If you're travelling up the M6, turn off at junction 36 and head for Kendal, then turn left on to the A590 and right on to the A5074 towards Bowness and Windermere. If that sounds complicated, locating the Masons Arms may be worse. Many small crossroads and junc-

The Masons Arms
Licensees: Helen & Nigel Stevenson
Strawberry Bank, Cartmel Fell, Cumbria
☎ Crosthwaite (044 88) 486
11-3; 6-11

McEwan 70/-, 80/-; Guest beers

Lunchtime & evening food. Self-catering accommodation. Families welcome. Outdoor drinking area.

tions in the Lake District have no signs and, on my first visit, I covered just about every inch of the land east of Lake Windermere before I found the pub. To avoid a similar fate, make for Bowland Bridge and, when you're actually on the bridge, you'll see the Masons Arms on the hillside high above you.

Despite any difficulties in reaching it, there is never a shortage of customers at the Masons Arms. Helen and Nigel Stevenson have run the pub for several years, but they retain their enthusiasm and their warm and friendly welcome for all. There is probably the best pub food in the Lake District, with a menu that includes daily specials and several vegetarian dishes. The British beer is excellent, but you can also choose one of the 130 or so foreign beers that the Stevensons keep; they import and wholesale many Belgian beers, but their stock covers just about every corner of the globe.

The pub has beams and stone floors, the main bar has a fine black-leaded fireplace, ladder-backed chairs and a carved oak settle with snarling dogs as arm-rests, and there's an oak-panelled lounge. There are wooden benches and tables outside where you can sit and enjoy the views over the Winster Valley, and even when the pub is crowded, the service remains fast and friendly. If you want to stay, there is self-catering accommodation available.

The Masons Arms is named after the Kendal Freemasons who used to meet there in secret when Freemasonry was illegal. You'll have no need of secret signs or handshakes – if you appreciate a good British pub, you won't find many better than this one.

When you're ready to move on further into the Lake District, give yourself a treat, and instead of ploughing down to Windermere and round the lake to Ambleside, take the ferry across to Hawkshead. You may have to wait for twenty minutes or so, but you'll have the pleasure of leaning on the rail and listening to the water lapping against the boat as you cross the lake, before you begin exploring the heart of the Lake District.

If you pass through Hawkshead and turn left at Outgate you will travel along narrow, winding, wooded country lanes past unsigned turnings to left and right. If your luck holds good, or if you ask the way, the lanes will lead you to the excellent, and bizarrely named, Drunken Duck at Barngates. It sits at a quiet crossroads roughly half-way between Ambleside, Hawkshead, Coniston and the Lang-

The Drunken Duck
Licensees: Peter & Stephanie Barton
Barngates, Ambleside, Cumbria
☎ Hawkshead 096 66 347
11-3; 5.30-10.30
(11 Friday, Saturday & summer)

Jennings Mild, Bitter; Marston Pedigree; Tetley Mild, Bitter; Theakston Bitter, XB; Guest beers

Lunchtime & evening food. Accommodation. Garden. Private fishing.

From the Drunken Duck at Barngates you can see across to the Lakes, and to the countryside all around

dales and has fine views over the surrounding countryside.

The menu often contains local specialities like potted char and Windermere trout, or, if you prefer, you can try and catch your own trout in the two private tarns behind the inn. Tickets are available by the day or by the evening. The inn has five bedrooms and is a pleasant place to stay, there is a residents' lounge and a dining room as well as the beamed bars with open fires on cold days.

The Drunken Duck owes its name to an incident in Victorian times, when the landlady discovered her ducks stretched out, apparently dead, in the road outside the pub. Deciding to cut her losses, she began to pluck them with the intention of serving them for dinner, but the 'dead' ducks did not like the treatment and began to revive. She discovered that a barrel of beer in the cellar had sprung a leak, and the beer had drained into the ducks' feeding ditch outside, making them dead drunk, but not dead. According to local lore, the landlady was so sorry for the half-plucked ducks that she fitted them out with knitted jerseys and kilts of Hawkshead yarn until their feathers grew again.

On leaving Barngates follow the narrow winding road north and take one of the roads into the Langdales from the main Coniston to Ambleside road. Turn into the village of Elterwater and you'll find another Lakeland classic, the Britannia. It looks out across a pocket-handkerchief village green with a wooden bench shaded by a tree. There is a terraced garden above the pub, where you are requested to 'keep the gate closed at all times to prevent the sheep from eating the plants', and there are tables outside the front of the inn, where you can sometimes sit and watch Morris Dancers on the green.

Inside is a beamed front bar with a slate fireplace and oak benches, a lounge with comfortable armchairs, and a smaller, more basic bar at the back, popular with locals and walkers. The inn serves good bar food and huge three- or four-course dinners – children overwhelmed by the size of the restaurant meals can order from the bar menu instead.

Close to the village green, the Britannia Inn at Elterwater is deservedly popular, especially in summer
Opposite: The magnificent setting of the Old Dungeon Ghyll Hotel

The Britannia Inn
Licensee: David Fry
Elterwater, Cumbria
☎ Langdale (096 67) 210
11-3; 6.30-10.30 (11 Friday & Saturday)

TRADITIONAL
Hartleys
DRAUGHT BEER

Bass Cask Bitter; Hartleys XB; Tetley Mild, Bitter; Bulmers Traditional Cider

Lunchtime & evening food. Accommodation. Garden. Families welcome.

The Britannia can be very busy in summer, but despite the crowds it retains its village inn atmosphere.

From Elterwater, the next stop is only a couple of miles away – follow the B5343 towards the Langdale Pikes, and at their foot you will find the Old Dungeon Ghyll Hotel. Dungeon Ghyll Force is nearby, an impressive waterfall which inspired the Wordsworth poem, 'The Idle Shepherd Boys'.

The walkers' bar in the Dungeon Ghyll Hotel is plainly furnished and decorated, with an enormous fire burning in an old black-leaded iron range. At weekends it will be crowded with walkers, climbers and some of the most enthusiastic (and least talented) singers you'll ever come across, and you're assured of a lively night! There's good hot food to sustain a weary hiker in the bar or the

hotel, and the accommodation is reasonably priced and comfortable. As well as a wide range of real ales, the bar also stocks a huge variety of snuffs.

The Langdales are spectacular enough, but the next stop on the way through Lakeland is in perhaps the most dramatic and impressive landscape of them all, Wasdale. There are two ways of getting there from Dungeon Ghyll; either don your hiking boots and take the direct route over the tops past Bow Fell and Scafell Pikes, or drive out of the Langdales and then take the road west, over the Wrynose and Hardknott Passes.

The road is single track with passing places – you will have to open a gate – and the gradients reach one in three in places. If you can cope with all that, you will be rewarded on a clear day by an absolutely stunning view, right out across West Cumbria and the sea as far as the Isle of Man. That is on a clear day; on a wild, wet and steel-grey winter's day you will be lucky to see your hand in front of your face and you will feel a great deal of sympathy, across the centuries, for the unfortunate Roman soldiers who manned the fort at Boot, just west of the Hardknott Pass.

Have a look at the Roman fort at Boot, then drop off the young and the young at heart at Boot Station for a ride down to the coast on the single-track, narrow-gauge Ravenglass & Eskdale railway, better known locally as La'al Ratty. You can collect them again at Ravenglass. Just up the coast is the Sellafield nuclear power and re-processing complex, but you may prefer the unspoilt delights of Wasdale and Wastwater, with the great mass of the Screes apparently frozen in motion as they slide into the icy depths of England's deepest lake.

On a still, clear, sunny morning, there cannot be a lovelier drive in the whole of England than the journey up Wasdale. There is not a ripple on the surface of the lake, and the water is so still that it is hard to tell where the reflections in the surface end and the far shore begins. The road runs alongside the northern shore of Wastwater, twisting and dipping past bracken and rock as it leads up to Wasdale Head. There, dwarfed by the bleak, dark masses of some of Lakeland's highest hills, Great Gable and Sca Fell, you will find the Wasdale Head Hotel.

The inn sits at the foot of tracks used by pack-horse traders and smugglers for centuries to cross over the Sty Head, Black Sail and

The Old Dungeon Ghyll Hotel
Licensee: N. J. Walmsley
Great Langdale, Cumbria
☎ Langdale (096 67) 272
11-3; 6-10.30 (11 Friday & Saturday)

Marston Burton Bitter, Pedigree; McEwan 80/-; Theakston Best Bitter, Old Peculier; Younger's No. 3

Lunchtime & evening food. Accommodation. Garden. Families welcome.

The Wasdale Head Hotel
Licensee: J. R. M. Carr
Wasdale Head, Cumbria
☎ Wasdale (094 06) 229
11-3; 5.30-11

Jennings Bitter; Theakston Best Bitter, Old Peculier

Lunchtime & evening food. Accommodation. Families welcome. Garden.

Burnmoor Passes. The slate-floored bar has a slighty spartan feel to it, appropriate to an inn that has long been a centre for rock-climbers. There is a wood-panelled main bar and, leading off it, a small room with a pool table. The bar is named after Will Ritson, a keen mountaineer who was the inn's first landlord and such a notorious pedlar of implausible stories that he was known as the world's biggest liar. An annual liars' competition is still held in his memory.

There is a good range of local beer and food available in the bar, or you can eat in the restaurant. If you are staying the night, there is a lovely little residents' bar, with beautiful

The Wasdale Head Hotel at the head of Wastwater, beneath the towering Cumbrian fells

oak panelling and three old oak benches, and a pleasantly old-fashioned residents' lounge. The inn also has self-catering accommodation available nearby.

Wasdale is well off the main tourist track; you can spend all day on the fells and scarcely see a soul. You will return tired but refreshed for a well-earned evening rest, eating, drinking and swopping tall stories in the Ritson tradition.

Before you move on, spare a few moments for a look at the tiny church of St Olaf. Claimed to be the smallest in England, it is hidden in a clump of yew trees a short walk from the inn. Then retrace your route past the Screes guarding Wastwater's cold depths and turn north towards the Solway Firth.

The first few miles of your journey north will be dominated by the sprawling Sellafield works on the coast. This Cumbrian coast has many miles of quiet beaches, but few people take the opportunity to bathe there these days. The beaches may or may not be contaminated, but not many are willing to take the risk.

When you reach Egremont, turn northeast towards Cockermouth, second only to Grasmere in the Wordsworth hierarchy. If you turn east on to the A66 just before Cockermouth, a short drive brings you to the shores of Bassenthwaite. Turn right just before the dual carriageway which runs by

The creeper-covered entrance to the Pheasant Inn at Bassenthwaite Lake. The Pheasant is an ideal base from which to explore the Northern Lakes

The Pheasant Inn
Licensee: W. E. Barrington-Wilson
Bassenthwaite Lake, Cumbria
☎ Bassenthwaite Lake (059 681) 234
11-3; 5.30-10.30

Lunchtime & evening food. Accommodation. Garden. Families welcome.

the lake, and there is the Pheasant Inn.

The Pheasant is a long, whitewashed, sixteenth-century building, with a lovely garden sloping down to the beech woods behind the inn. There is a small two-roomed bar, with oak settles and walls that have the patina of old copper, either from yacht varnish or centuries of tobacco smoke. You can eat lunch in the large lounge that looks out over the gardens and the food is home-made and delicious. The Pheasant is a very pleasant base from which to explore the Northern Lakes, but it is very popular, so book well in advance if you are planning a stop there.

When you are rested and refreshed, take the A66 east past Keswick, at the head of Derwentwater nestling beneath the towering slopes of Skiddaw. The summit is a stiff test for the less-than-fit but the views in all directions make the suffering worthwhile!

To the
Scottish Borders

'A bouquet of old trees stands round a white
farmhouse, and from a neighbouring dell you can
see smoke rising and leaves rustling in the breeze.
Straight above, the hills climb a thousand feet into
the air.'

'ST IVES'
R L STEVENSON

The Hare & Hounds, Talkin, offers one of the warmest welcomes in England

Though the Lake District can be swamped with summer visitors, the Cumbrian slopes of the Pennines a few miles to the east are little known and usually very quiet. You can spend a pleasant day exploring the back roads which run roughly parallel to the M6, but make sure that by late afternoon your wanderings have led you to the village of Talkin, just east of the B6413, three miles from Brampton, where you will find the Hare & Hounds.

It was once used as a stopping point for monks on their way from Armathwaite to Lanercost Priory, and it now provides the perfect resting-place for travellers on the way to Scotland. The pub is lovely, with beams, antiques, log fires, good beer, excellent food and really comfortable bedrooms for an overnight stop; but what really singles it out is the warmth and friendliness of the licensees.

The Stewarts' friendly welcome is legendary, and they and their staff really do seem to take pleasure in serving their customers – after the morose and off-hand treatment you can often find in pubs, the Hare & Hounds is a delight. Its lunchtime openings are limited to holiday times but this is a pub that should definitely not be missed. The food is very reasonably priced and there's a children's menu at rock-bottom prices as well. If you stay the night, you can sprint down the road and take an icy dip in Talkin Tarn before breakfast or you can have a round of golf on the nearby Brampton course.

The Hare & Hounds
Licensees: Joan & Les Stewart
Talkin Village, nr Carlisle, Cumbria
☎ Brampton (069 77) 3456/7
12-2.30 (July, August & Bank Holidays only); 7-10.30 (11 Friday & Saturday)

TRADITIONAL
Hartleys
DRAUGHT BEER

Hartleys XB; Theakston Best Bitter, XB, Old Peculier; Bulmers Traditional Cider

Lunchtime & evening food. Accommodation. Families welcome. Garden. Camping nearby.

From Talkin, head north to Brampton, turning right on to the A69 towards Newcastle, but at the end of the town, fork left on to the minor road that leads you to Lanercost and Banks. Lanercost Priory sits in an idyllic setting by the River Irthing, a picture of peace and tranquillity. In the past that peace has been rudely disturbed when Scots raiders sacked the Priory, as the Chronicle of Lanercost relates.

Border raiding was a Scottish national occupation from the eleventh century onwards. In 1138 William, son of Duncan, raided with an army down the Eden valley and 'the whole land was laid waste and no rank or age and neither sex was spared'. The raids grew very common after the Scots' victory at Bannockburn in 1314; men and children were killed, women taken into slavery and vast quantities of livestock were stolen. The Scots would also negotiate ransoms with the frightened townsfolk and villagers, taking cash and valuables in return for sparing the crops and the people.

Chains of castles were built across the North, supplemented with fortified houses in an attempt to control the Scots. After the 'shameful peace' recognising Robert the Bruce as King of Scotland in the early fourteenth century, the worst of the organised raiding ceased, but border reivers and moss-troopers, bandits from the hills, continued to terrorise the unfortunate Borderers right up to the Act of Union in 1603.

From Lanercost's now peaceful ruins, take the road up through Banks. There is a steep climb until just past the village, then the road levels out and runs right alongside Hadrian's Wall. The Wall was originally built of turf and later reconstructed from stone. Here you might stop and look at the Milecastle, and a little further on, as the road bends away from the Wall, there is a fine stretch still standing. You can walk along the top of it, following its line with your eyes as it snakes over the distant hills.

As you travel anywhere in the region of the Wall, you cannot fail to notice how well built many of the farms and houses are. The presence of such a ready supply of perfectly dressed stone was too much of a temptation to farmers in the area, and much of Hadrian's Wall is now visible as large rectangular stones in farmhouse walls.

You can follow the Wall east as far as Gilsland before taking the B6318 back to the north-west. It is worth making a detour from it to look at the Roman fort at Bewcastle, one of the many forts north of Hadrian's Wall,

Seals of approval at the window of the Hare & Hounds, Talkin

dating from the time when the Romans still retained ambitions to rule the whole of Britain. Then follow the road over Arthur Seat and down into the steep-walled valley of Liddel Water, before crossing the Esk into Canonbie.

The award-winning Riverside Inn at Canonbie on the banks of the Esk

Just after you cross the river, you will see the Riverside Inn on your right, looking out across the broad, softly wooded valley of the Esk. It is an award-winning pub and restaurant, and a spell in its comfortable oak-beamed bar, reached through an arch from the lounge, with an open fire burning in the stone fireplace, will convince you of its merits. If you need further proof, try some of the unusual and delicious bar food, all home-made, with much use of fresh local ingredients. You can also eat in the restaurant, where the food is equally good and even more adventurous.

The inn has accommodation, so you can break your journey for a few days if you wish, look around the Borders, seek out Robbie Burns connections, or fish for salmon in the Esk – the inn can arrange permits. If you are just there for a drink and a bite to eat, you can take them at tables under the trees outside or in the carefully furnished rooms inside, where, apart from the conversation, the loudest noise you hear will be the ticking of the long-case clock.

From Canonbie, take the A7 north to Langholm, then turn off on to the B709 and follow it all the way up Eskdale. The road crosses and re-crosses the Esk, climbing through its beautiful valley, the river far below, the mountains rising steadily all around. The journey is through increasingly heavily forested hills, but conifer forests are not always blocks of uniform dark green; here the deciduous larches break up the monotony with their changing colour and their graceful outlines.

Leaving the Esk behind, climb up to the summit through Castle O'er Forest and drop down into the valley of the White Esk, where you can see the mountains stretching away to the north-west as far as the eye can see. On my visit the tops were capped with snow, even in mid-October! Just past Eskdalemuir, you will come across the bizarre sight of a Tibetan pagoda, built for the Tibetan centre there, in the middle of a Scottish glen.

Now you climb up again, to the head-waters of the Esk, and cross the watershed into the catchment of the Tweed. You pass Loch Tima, and then drop into a series of

The Riverside Inn
Licensees: Robert & Susan Phillips
Canonbie, Borders
☎ Canonbie (054 15) 295
11-2.30; 6.30-11. Closed on Sunday

Broughton Merlins Ale; Theakston Best Bitter

Lunchtime & evening food. Restaurant. Accommodation. Families welcome. Garden. Fishing permits available.

glens surrounded by hills, with cattle grazing and a scatter of lonely farms. In autumn, rowan berries make a vivid red splash in an otherwise green and brown landscape.

Climb up once more by a steep, narrow road that twists and turns, hugging the mountain side, then breast the top, and you will find yourself looking down into a long glaciated valley. You pass an old stone sheepfold that will soon be submerged by trees, a reflection of the change coming throughout Britain, as the uplands are turned from sheep farming to the exclusive preserve of forestry and field sports.

The Gordon Arms, Yarrow, meeting-place of Sir Walter Scott and the 'Ettrick Shepherd' in 1830

Drop down to the bridge across Yarrow Water and in front of you is the Gordon Arms Hotel. A plaque on the wall proclaims: 'At this inn in the autumn of 1830, Sir Walter Scott and the Ettrick shepherd met and parted for the last time.'

The Gordon Arms was first granted a full licence when James Hogg, the 'Ettrick Shepherd', proposed it and Sir Walter Scott, the local magistrate, granted it. Since the two men regularly met and drank there, the decision to grant it a licence may not have been wholly disinterested. It had been an ale-house for many years before, a place where drovers and pack-horse traders could pause for refreshment and to exchange news of the outside world. The racks on which pack-horse saddles were hung can still be seen in the passage through to the games room.

There is also a cosy bar, a lounge and a dining-room, which doubles as a room for

The Gordon Arms
Licensees: Bill & Myra Rowe
Yarrow, Borders
☎ Yarrow (0750) 82222
11-11 seven days a week

Broughton Greenmantle Ale

Lunchtime & evening food. Accommodation. Families welcome.

socials and ceilidhs. The lounge is an interesting example of '1950s modern', not really in keeping with the age and traditions of the pub, but the atmosphere and the welcome are as warm as you could wish for, a perfect antidote for the bleak cold of the hills in winter. As well as lunch and an evening meal, you can stop here for breakfast if you are passing. Stay at the pub and you can have free fishing on the Yarrow or the Ettrick. Non-residents may buy fishing permits.

You are very close here to Traquair House, the oldest inhabited building in Scotland, dating from 1100, with a brewhouse producing some of Scotland's finest and strongest ale. You can drink it in bottle in the Gordon Arms, but Traquair House itself is well worth a visit and is only a few miles out of your way along the road that runs north from beside the pub. In the summer season, you can visit the House between 10.30 a.m. and 5.30 p.m. seven days a week for a modest admission fee and you can sample the Traquair beer in the tea-rooms at the House, from noon to 5 p.m.

With or without a visit to Traquair House, take the road west from the Gordon Arms down past St Mary's Loch, across which Mary Queen of Scots is supposed to have rowed on her way to Hermitage Castle. The loch curls away into the hills and our road branches off to the right towards Tweedsmuir. Climb up once more, this time past the huge wall of Meggat Reservoir. It is odd that a country awash with lochs should have the need of so many reservoirs; perhaps, like Wales, the water of Scotland flows too freely to England.

Climb up a single-track road with passing places, cross the summit through a very narrow rocky gorge between the mountains rising sheer on either side and then drop down a steep hill with a spectacular view of Talla Reservoir sparkling below you, hemmed in by the mountains.

After crossing the Tweed, at the junction turn right up the hill and after a couple of miles you reach the Crook Inn. The name suggests a shepherds' inn, and it dates from the sixteenth century, but from the outside it looks like a classic piece of 1930s architecture. The curved steel and glass windows, the veneered doors and the lettering could all have been made for a 1930s cinema; but pass through the plushly carpeted interior, open a door and suddenly you are stepping back three hundred years.

The pub was built in 1590, and it is said

The Crook Inn
Licensee: Bill MacDowell
Tweedsmuir, Borders
☎ Tweedsmuir (089 97) 272
11-2.30; 6-11 (Tea & coffee available all day)

Broughton Greenmantle Ale

Lunchtime & evening food. Restaurant. Accommodation. Garden. Fishing permits available. Families welcome.

One of the unusual features inside the Crook Inn

to be Scotland's oldest licensed inn, with a licence dating from 1604. The bar was once the kitchen, and there is a vast central fireplace, which you can walk right around. The floor is stone-flagged and you will settle happily into the wooden seats to enjoy the warmth and comfort of this friendly, traditional bar. Robbie Burns knew and used the inn; it sits by the old Edinburgh to Dumfries road, used by Burns in his occupation as an exciseman. He wrote his poem 'Willie Wastle' while staying here.

The Crook Inn was originally a drovers' inn. For centuries the hills of the Borders saw the passage of hundreds of thousands of cattle every year, driven south to fatten on the stubble of the English harvest. The relative affluence of England and the insatiable appetite of the armed forces for salt beef created a demand for Scottish and Welsh cattle that made it economic for drovers to bring beasts from the farthest corners of the highlands and islands to sell at great cattle fairs in England. A chain of dealers would trade the beasts on, and the majority would end their days in the great market of Smithfield in London. To ensure the stock arrived at market in good condition, the pace of a drove was wearisomely slow, perhaps only ten to twelve miles a day. The drove would halt at midday to graze, and would pass the night at a 'stance', where grazing and water were available.

The droves created 'greenways' and drove roads across the uplands, and inns in high and lonely places provided food and shelter for the drover and his beasts, though many slept rough with their animals, existing on a diet of crowdie (a kind of oatmeal porridge mixed with blood bled from one of the beasts), and a little whisky from a ram's horn container.

Sir Walter Scott, whom we came across in connection with the Gordon Arms, knew and wrote often about the droving trade. His most famous creation, Rob Roy, was in fact a highland gangster who exacted protection money for allowing drovers to pass unmolested through his territory, and Scott's story 'Two Drovers' captures well the flavour of the trade:

'The highlanders are masters of this difficult trade of droving, which seems to suit them as well as the trade of war. It affords exercise for all their habits of patient endurance and active exertion. They are required to know perfectly the drove roads which lie over the wildest tracts of the country and to avoid as much as possible the highways which distress the feet of the bullocks and the turnpikes which annoy the spirit of the drover; whereas on the broad green or grey track

Opposite: The Castle Inn, Dirleton, the first stop on the old coaching road from Edinburgh to Dunbar

which leads across the pathless moor, the herd not only move at ease and without taxation, but, if they mind their business, may pick up a mouthful of food by the way.'

There were drovers' inns throughout the borders of England, Wales and Scotland. Many have now fallen into decay or reverted to use as private houses or farms. A few still remain, and we shall come to one or two when we reach the Yorkshire Dales. Here, as at Yarrow, is a pub that served both the drovers and the newer trade of coaching that followed the construction of the turnpikes, the first solidly made roads in Britain since the Romans left our shores.

Follow the road north to Broughton, then take the B road through Biggar to Carnwath, where you pick up the A70 towards Edinburgh. You are now out of the mountains and into more gentle, rolling country with wide open vistas to the Pentland Hills which run parallel to the road. Straight ahead of you are the first views of Arthur's Seat and the Edinburgh skyline in the far distance.

As you near the outskirts of Edinburgh, turn off the A70 at the Balerno sign. The village main street is a no-go area for cars, so you will need to use the car-parks, which are signed. Though there has been development all around it, the heart of Balerno remains very much a country village, with a winding street of stone houses containing the Grey Horse, very much a village pub.

One unfortunate aspect of this tradition is that the Grey Horse is closed on Sundays, but it is well worth a visit during the week to enjoy the atmosphere and character, both of which owe much to the character of the landlady, Mrs Brow. It is uncompromisingly old-fashioned; that means no food, no families, no frills. The interior is wood-panelled and there are some splendid engraved glass mirrors, but what makes this pub a classic is that it is a timeless, unspoilt village local, an oasis of permanence in a fast-changing world.

It would be a rare visitor to Scotland who did not want to spend some time in Edinburgh. It would win my vote as the finest city in Britain, and even out of the Festival season there is still enough to see and do to keep the most energetic visitor fully occupied. Take in the Castle, the Royal Mile and Edinburgh's many other delights, and when you have seen your fill of 'Auld Reekie', travel out to the east on the A1, and then take the road to North Berwick, which leads

The Grey Horse
Licensee: Mrs Brow
Main Street, Balerno, Lothian
☎ (031) 449 3092

Belhaven 60/-, 80/-

first past a power station and a mine and then into beautiful coastal country. The road drops down to run right alongside the Firth of Forth, past sand dunes covered with gorse. You pass a succession of fine old houses, one estate seeming to succeed another without a break.

Turn off the North Berwick road at the Dirleton sign and in the heart of Dirleton you will find the Castle Inn, looking out over the village green to the castle itself. The castle was built in 1225, and was last used as a place of defence during the Civil War, when Cromwell took it in 1650. For centuries, Dirleton consisted of the castle and nothing else; the village and the church were at Gullane along the coast. Then, just as at Kenfig in Wales, the sea took a hand. The farmland surrounding the village was engulfed by sand around the turn of the seventeenth century, and a new church and a new village were built close to the castle.

The Castle Inn was an important coaching inn, the first stop out of Edinburgh on the old road to Dunbar. Now it is a quieter, less bustling place, an excellent village local and a fine place to stay, not too far out of Edinburgh, yet with the peace of the countryside all around. There is a comfortable lounge with a big open fire, a public bar with some fine old engraved mirrors and another open fire, and a pool room. Have a meal and a drink, stay the night, and on waking you will look out across the village green to the castle ruins, an appropriate start to a day that will take you past more castles than you would think possible.

The Castle Inn
Licensee: Douglas Stewart
Dirleton, Lothian
☎ Dirleton (062 085) 221
11-2.30; 5-11 (midnight Friday & Saturday); 11-11 Sunday

McEwan 80/-

Lunchtime & evening food. Accommodation. Families welcome. Garden.

The bar of the Olde Ship Inn at Seahouses is crammed with lovingly-polished nautical memorabilia

Leaving Dirleton, continue along the coast road towards Dunbar. Just after North Berwick, the road runs right alongside the Firth, and you can look across to the rocky islands just off the shore.

The whole of this coast from Edinburgh to Newcastle was heavily fortified with castles against the threat of raids from the sea by the Norsemen and from the land by the Scots. As well as the castles, there are fortified houses right across the English Borders, either castles in miniature, or houses with a Pele Tower in which the inhabitants and their neighbours hoped to resist the Scots for long enough for them to tire of their sport or for help to arrive.

The boundary between England and Scotland was a movable feast for centuries, and the two countries were in a permanent state of hostility until the Act of Union in 1603. Even this did not entirely heal the scars, and the Jacobite rebellions of 1715 and 1745 saw the Scots once more marching into England, though the rebellions ended in the terrible slaughter of the Scots at Culloden, a grim end to centuries of brutal encounters.

The road now rejoins the A1 and runs close to the coast down into Northumbria. Above Berwick, the road follows the cliffs, high above the North Sea. To the south of the border, Holy Island comes into view, a place well worth visiting, both for its marvellous setting and its history. Holy Island lies just off the coast, approached by a causeway which is submerged at high tide. On the island is a castle, and also the remains of Lindisfarne Priory, our earliest Christian site. Looking south from Holy Island you can see the magnificent castle at Bamburgh, and out to sea from there the Farne Islands, breeding site for thousands of puffins and many other species of sea bird.

Turn off the A1 on the B1342 towards Bamburgh. The road drops down to the sea and climbs over a headland from where there is the majestic sight of Bamburgh Castle ahead of you. It is a magnificent and imposing castle, one of the few that are still in excellent condition. The road, which runs right under its walls, takes you south along the coast to the village of Seahouses, where the first classic pub back in England is waiting.

The Olde Ship at Seahouses sits above a tiny harbour full of local fishing boats. From the jetty you can take boat trips out to the Farne Islands. The nautical theme is maintained in the Olde Ship, which has one of the most remarkable bars you will come across, bulging at the seams with nautical memora-

The Olde Ship Inn
Licensee: Mr & Mrs A. C. Glen
Seahouses, Northumberland
☎ Seahouses (0665) 720200
11-3; (12-2 Sunday); 6-10.30 (winter) 11 (summer)

McEwan 80/-; Newcastle Bitter; Exhibition; Younger's Scotch

Lunchtime & evening food. Accommodation. Garden.

Opposite: The village of Netherton in the heart of Northumberland

bilia. There are ships' figureheads, sextants, portholes, a diver's helmet, a binnacle and heaven knows what else, all polished till they shine like jewels. The landlord and a team of volunteers polish everything every Sunday; visit the pub and you will realise what a labour of love that is.

The pub, which has been in the same family for seventy-five years, is a fine place for visitors and a great local pub as well. The ship theme is carried on through every room in the building, and even the windows are stained glass with a ship motif. You can eat in the dining-room in the evening or have a lunch in the bar which might include locally caught crab or fish.

There is a terrace, a garden with rustic fence poles and a summer-house, all looking out over the harbour, and you can try your hand at the traditional game of quoits.

The Star at Netherton, surrounded by gardens, but at the heart of bleak and isolated countryside

L eaving Seahouses you follow the same road towards Alnwick. Cross the A1 and drop down into Alnwick where, if your appetite for them is not already sated, you can take a look at the castle. Then take the road to Rothbury. Climb up into Rothbury Forest, where the early warning radar stations stand sentinel on the hills around you. The coast was once dominated by the castles that kept watch towards the east; now it is policed from metal towers inland.

Descend into a valley with a graceful stone viaduct and, inevitably, a ruined castle, this time Edlingham. You also cross the Devil's Causeway at this point, a track that ran all the way from Hexham to Berwick. Then cross over the main road from Coldstream to Morpeth and climb up to the top of the hill, where you are rewarded with spectacular views of the Cheviots to the north and the Pennines to west and south.

Pass through Rothbury, another very stately, stone-built town with a long green running through the middle, and follow the Otterburn signs, travelling up Coquetdale before turning off at Thropton to Netherton. Halfway to Netherton you cross the Roman road from Rochester (Bremenium) to the Devil's Causeway at Thrunton. The country hereabouts is bleak and very isolated, and it requires no great stretch of imagination to see Border reivers and moss-troopers sweeping down on these isolated farms and villages.

The Star at Netherton is a stone building, with an immaculate red gravel forecourt and carefully tended gardens. On the hill opposite is a cock-fighting pit, mercifully disused. The Star was built around the time of

The Star
Licensee: W. W. W. Morton
Netherton,
Northumberland
☎ Rothbury (0669) 238
11-3; 6-10.30 (opening hours may vary)

EST.ᴰ 1742

Whitbread Castle Eden

the First World War and has not been altered since. There is no bar, just a serving hatch, with a public room with slatted wooden benches and a fine brewery mirror, while for Mr Morton's 'very select customers' there is a cosy little snug behind the serving hatch.

There are absolutely no concessions to changing times here. Like the Grey Horse at Balerno, the Star is a no-food, no-children, no-fruit machine, no-muzak, no-nonsense establishment. It has been in the same family since it was built, and is well worth a visit as a reminder of an earlier, less frenzied age than our own.

L eaving Netherton, retrace your route towards Rothbury but turn right at Thropton towards Otterburn, an area thick with Roman roads and camps. Turn left in Otterburn on to the A68, the Roman Dere Street, which takes you south to Corbridge, an important Roman site with a magnificent bridge over the Tyne. Shortly before Corbridge, you cross the line of Hadrian's Wall, though the only visible evidence of it here is the vallum and the military road.

From Corbridge, take the B6307, and then the B6306 south. As you clear Slaley Forest, Derwent reservoir lies below you. The road skirts Blanchland Moor and brings you to the stunningly beautiful village of Blanchland, named for the 'white monks' who occupied the ruined abbey at its core.

The Lord Crewe Arms
Licensees: J. Stephens & C. Simpson
Blanchland,
County Durham
☎ Blanchland (043 475) 251
11-3; 6-10.30 (11 Friday, Saturday & summer). Open all day for tea and coffee

Vaux Samson

Lunchtime & evening food. Restaurant. Accommodation. Garden. Families welcome.

Armour in the Lord Crewe Arms at Blanchland, once the dwelling of the Abbot of Blanchland Abbey

The abbey was established in 1165 and flourished until the Dissolution of the Monasteries, when it passed into secular hands. This was not the only disaster to befall the abbey; in 1296 it was sacked by the Scots in an incident celebrated in a poem 'The Blanchland Bells'. The Scots were pillaging the area, but passed by the abbey on a moonless night without realising it was there. At first light, the monks gave thanks to God for sparing them by ringing the abbey bells. Unfortunately for them, the Scots were still within earshot, the sound being carried to them on the wind, and they turned back and destroyed the church and the bells that had betrayed it.

The abbey again fell into ruins after the Dissolution, but the village was rebuilt in the eighteenth century, when it was formally laid out as a model village. At his death the then Lord Crewe left the village to a trust to ensure that it remained unaltered, and for two hundred years nothing has been allowed to harm or change the village. As a result it is a magnificent place to visit.

The pub at its heart, the Lord Crewe Arms, was originally the abbot's dwelling. The main entrance leads you into what was once the kitchen, with a stone fireplace massive enough for an ox-roast. In the lounge there is an ingle-nook with a 'priest hole' and a chimney appearing to stretch away to infinity. The Crypt Bar, as the name suggests, is a stone-flagged arch-roofed crypt, as full of character as the rest of this superb building. Behind the Crewe Arms are the gardens, once the cloisters of the abbey, where you can walk and enjoy the solitude in the footsteps of the monks of Blanchland.

Among its many other attractions, the Lord Crewe is claimed to have a ghost, Dorothy Forster, Lord Crewe's wife and sister of Tom Forster, general of the Jacobite forces in the rebellion of 1715. He proved unequal to the task, surrendering to the government without a fight, but escaped from Newgate Prison three days before his trial for treason, thanks to his sister's courage and quick wit. She rode to London disguised as a servant and managed to obtain duplicate keys to the prison, with which he made his escape. Tom Forster fled to the safety of France, and it is the ghost of Dorothy which is said to pace the Bamburgh Room of the Lord Crewe Arms, waiting for news of her brother.

The Lord Crewe has comfortable rooms, some with four-poster beds, and the restaurant offers traditional English dishes, the ideal accompaniment to a spell at a most traditional English inn.

To the Yorkshire Moors and Dales

'All round the horizon there is this same line of sinuous wave-like hills; the scoops into which they fall only revealing other hills beyond, of similar colour and shape, crowned with wild, bleak moors . . .'

THE LIFE OF CHARLOTTE BRONTË
ELIZABETH GASKELL

The journey down the coast, across the North Yorkshire Moors and through the Yorkshire Dales will take us through some of the most beautiful country in Britain, which is in direct contrast to the ugliness of industrial Teesside.

Turn off the A1 through Darlington, and as you drive past Middlesbrough on your way east towards Saltburn-by-the-Sea, you have on your left the giant ICI Wilton works and a thousand chimneys belching out a thousand different kinds of smoke. To your right is some measure of relief, the beginnings of the North Yorkshire Moors stretching up towards the unmistakable peak of Roseberry Topping.

Saltburn is typical of the resorts that sprang up around the coast in the nineteenth century in response to the new fashion for seaside holidays. Its stately Victorian houses line the cliff-top, looking down into the cove where you will find the Ship Inn. It stands on the beach, surrounded by the small boats drawn up on the shingle. At low tide you can walk along the sandy beach towards the pier and enjoy the views out to sea and towards the steep red cliffs along the coast.

The Ship has a tile-floored bar with rough wooden tables and an open fire. The Drybrough beer is served through Scottish-style tall founts. There is a light, airy lounge and a dining-room where you can eat local sea-food. On a fine evening, you can take your drink out on to the terrace and gaze out over the sea. Industrial Teesside could be a thousand miles away instead of just around the corner.

The Ship Inn
Licensees: Bill & Elisabeth Jack
Saltburn-by-the-Sea, Cleveland
☎ Guisborough (0287) 22361
11-3; 6-10.30 (11 Friday & Saturday)

Drybrough Pentland, Eighty

Lunchtime & evening food. Families welcome.

Boats drawn up beneath the Royal at Runswick Bay, one of the many lovely fishing villages on the Yorkshire coast

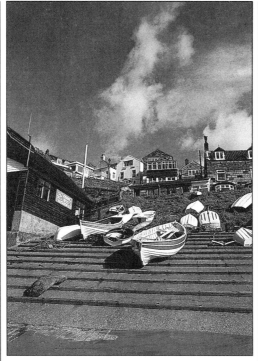

Travelling down the coast towards Whitby, you pass a score of lovely villages, each clinging to the steep cliffs above the sea. This is Captain Cook country, and one of the villages you pass is Staithes, where he was born. A little further south, turn off down to the village of Runswick Bay. Here the houses seem to huddle together for protection from the winter storms, and at their heart you will find the Royal.

The Royal has a small back bar with an open fire and a collection of old photographs and artefacts connected with the village. There are pictures of the lifeboats and their crews and even a bit of the propeller from a First World War aeroplane that crashed nearby. The front bar opens on to a terrace where you can sit and look out over the bay to the cliffs at Kettleness. You can also enjoy the views from the upstairs restaurant, where the menu includes pheasant and quail. However, you may wish to save game for meals further inland and here enjoy the locally caught sea-food, lobster and crab instead.

Following the coast south you come to Whitby, an historic town with much to offer the visitor: more Captain Cook connections, a whalebone arch at the entrance to the town, a small harbour packed with fishing boats, a ruined abbey reached by a seemingly endless flight of steps, and the place where Bram Stoker's Dracula made his landing in England.

The Royal
Licensee: Allan McConnell
Runswick Bay, North Yorkshire
11.30-3 (2.30 winter);
6 (7 winter)-11

Camerons Strongarm

Food lunchtime & evening. Restaurant. Garden. Families welcome.

Our route now lies inland across the moors to Pickering, but you may wish first to see the beautiful village of Robin Hood's Bay or even travel down the coast as far as Scarborough, with its castle and annual cricket festival in early September. If you do, however, you will miss one of the strangest sights in the whole of Britain, the radar early-warning 'golf balls' on Fylingdales Moor. Driving past these three huge white spheres set in a sea of heather moorland is like passing through some weird lunar landscape; it is quite a relief when they drop out of sight behind you.

Further down the Pickering road, you pass through the village of Saltersgate, its name a reminder of the vital function that salt used to have in the lives of every community. Before the rock salt mines of Cheshire were discovered, all our salt was obtained from evaporation of sea water in salt pans around the coast. The salt from these pans was carried all over the country by wagon or pack-horse, and was used to preserve the meat – salt beef or salt pork – of animals slaughtered in the late autumn. The routes by which the salters carried the precious commodity from the coast inland were called salters' gates.

The most famous customer of the Blacksmiths Arms at Lastingham, in his last resting place
Opposite: The church and pub are at the heart of the village of Lastingham

At Pickering you may enjoy a break to look at the castle or take a trip on the narrow-gauge North Yorkshire Moors Railway, back up through Goathland to Grosmont. When you are ready, take the A170 west towards Helmsley and turn off through Cropton to Lastingham. This area of Yorkshire is full of immaculate villages with stone-walled houses under red pantiled roofs. Lastingham is a pretty village, with the beautiful church of St Mary Lastingham at its head. The church was built in 1078 on the site of the Celtic monastery, shrine of St Cedd.

Across the road from the church, as in so many other English villages, is the other pillar of English social life, the pub. The Blacksmiths Arms has another church connection: two hundred years ago its landlord was an impecunious parson, whose explanation was that he needed the extra money to feed and clothe his large family.

There is a small dining area off the main bar, with its boarded ceiling, old wood settles and fine black-leaded range, but the star attraction is in a glass case at the side of the fire. Donald the Superduck was a much-loved family pet, sire of three broods a year with the help of his mate Daisy, but unfortunately

The Blacksmiths Arms
Licensee: R. F. Taylor
Lastingham,
North Yorkshire
☎ Lastingham (075 15) 247
11-2.30 (11.30-2 winter); 6.30-10.30
(11 Friday, Saturday & summer)

Matthew Brown Mild, Bitter, John Peel; Theakston Best Bitter, Old Peculier

Food lunchtime and evening. Garden. Families welcome. Accommodation (not suitable for children).

The Star at Harome, a pub smothered with beautiful flowers in summer and famous for its delicious food

Donald was so tame that he was a literal sitting duck for the dog which killed him. He is now stuffed, forever in the bar, while Daisy has a new non-pub-going mate.

From Lastingham, take the road through the picture-postcard village of Hutton-le-Hole, before returning to the A170. Turning off at Beadlam you come to Harome, with its fourteenth-century pub, the Star, nestling under a thatched roof. The white-washed walls are covered in flowers, and you can sit out either on the terrace at the front or in the lovely garden behind the pub. Inside is a bar with high-backed settles, an open fireplace and a fine collection of furniture by 'Mousey Thompson', the Kilburn craftsman whose pieces always carry the unmistakable 'signature' of a small, carved mouse somewhere upon them.

What brings people from far and wide to the Star is not the thatched roof or the furniture, however, but the food. The bar lunches include fine cheeses, meats, pâtés and smoked salmon as well as a range of unusual and delicious sandwiches. Not many pubs would be willing or able to put on prawn or chicken curry sandwiches; the Star does, and they are excellent. In the evening, the _à la carte_ restaurant offers a range of dishes that might include tiny shrimps in lobster and anchovy sauce, and fillet steak cooked with smoked oysters, brandy and cream.

You can drink your coffee or even have a private party in a room high in the rafters of

The Star
Licensee: A. D. Bowron
Harome, North Yorkshire
☎ Helmsley (0439) 70397
11.30-2.30; 6.30-10.30
(11 Friday, Saturday & summer)

Camerons Lion Bitter; Theakston Best Bitter, Old Peculier; Vaux Samson

Food lunchtimes except Christmas Day. _A la carte_ restaurant Tuesday to Saturday (closed in January). Garden. Families welcome.

the Star, but there is no accommodation; for that you will have to travel just a little further.

From Harome take the minor road through Nunnington, perhaps pausing for a look at Nunnington Hall, owned by the National Trust, then turn right and go right again when you reach the main road. In a short while you will find a turning on the left that leads to the village of Oswaldkirk, perched on a wooded hillside, looking out over the valley below.

Oswaldkirk was mentioned in the 'Domesday Book', though the Malt Shovel there is not quite as old. It was built as the Manor House in 1610 and converted to a coaching inn in the eighteenth century. The front of the pub stands right on the roadside, but at the back there is a spacious garden that even includes a box maze. You are unlikely to get lost in it, however; it is only a few feet across and about eighteen inches high!

Inside there is a front bar with a huge ingle-nook fireplace, a lounge and a small bar with an open fire and two high-backed settles. You can eat either in the bar or in the restaurant. The menu is the same in both, the food is made from fresh local ingredients and is excellent. Whether you want to stay a few nights while you explore the area, or just to break your journey before travelling on towards the Yorkshire Dales, the Malt Shovel makes a good stopping point.

The Malt Shovel
Licensee: Ian Pickering
Oswaldkirk, North Yorkshire
☎ Ampleforth (043 93) 461
11-2.30; 6.30-10.30
(11 Friday, Saturday & summer)

Samuel Smith Old Brewery Bitter

Food every lunchtime and evening (except Monday). Garden. Families welcome. Accommodation.

The imposing facade of the Malt Shovel at Oswaldkirk

When you leave Oswaldkirk, take the road north to Helmsley, with its castle guarding the entrance to Ryedale, then take the B1257 running north and turn off to Rievaulx Abbey. Rievaulx was one of the great Cistercian abbeys, with lands stretching right across Yorkshire. At the time of Henry VIII's Dissolution of the Monasteries the lands were confiscated and the buildings fell into ruins, but the remains of the abbey and its beautiful setting by the Rye are enough to make even the most world-weary tourist catch his breath.

From Rievaulx you should retrace the route to Helmsley and then follow the A170 as it makes its breath-taking hairpin descent of Sutton Bank, where gliders and hang-gliders hover like hawks on the thermals rising up the steep face of the Hambleton Hills. You are now so close to the walled city of York that it would be unforgivable to pass by without paying it a visit.

York was one of the principal cities of Roman Britain, the capital of a Viking kingdom that stretched from the East Coast to Dublin, a great medieval city, and is the home of one of Britain's most magnificent buildings, York Minster. It is worth taking some time to enjoy the bustle of the city, as a change from the peace of the countryside, before getting back on the country pub route again. The Viking king Eric Bloodaxe set out from York to the battle of Stainmore, a battle from which he never returned. We too must travel to the bleak, inhospitable fells around Stainmore, to reach the highest and loneliest pub in Britain.

Whichever way you travel, north or south, there is one pub right on the roof of England – the Pennines – that you should not miss. The Tan Hill Inn, at 1,732 feet above sea level, is the highest inn in England. It is situated about four miles south of the summit of the notorious Stainmore Pass on the A66, invariably one of the first roads to be blocked by the winter snows, but to reach it requires a round trip of several miles to the east or the west.

One way to approach Tan Hill is from the east through Richmond, up Swaledale to Reeth; then fork right into Arkengarthdale and keep going. It can also be reached from the A66 just west of Stainmore Summit (take the Barras/South Stainmore turning; Tan Hill is signed off that road); from the A685 Brough–Kirkby Stephen road (follow the Kaber or South Stainmore signs); or from just west of Keld in Upper Swaledale. There is

Opposite: The bleak moorland setting of the Tan Hill Inn, Britain's highest inn

Tan Hill Inn
Licensees: Alec & Margaret Baines
Keld, nr Richmond, North Yorkshire
☎ Bowes (0833) 28246
11-3; 6-11. Open all day for tea and coffee

Theakston Bitter, XB, Old Peculier

Food (lunchtime and evening until 8.30). Accommodation. Families welcome. Garden (10,000 acres!).

also a (very) rough road from Bowes across Sleightholme Moor; use it only if you have every confidence in your suspension . . . or if you are driving someone else's car! From whatever direction you approach, you will think that you must have missed Tan Hill and that no one could possibly have built a pub in such a desolate spot – but you have not, and someone did!

Tan Hill sits right on the Pennine Way, at the crossroads of tracks that were ancient when the Romans invaded Britain. Drovers, pack-horse traders and the coal miners who worked the numerous fell-top pits all once used the inn. There is nothing luxurious about Tan Hill's thick stone walls, flagged floors and wooden benches, but countless lost and weary travellers down the centuries have been grateful for the shelter offered by this lonely inn, and for the warmth from its blazing open fire. Now it sits in splendid isolation, its nearest neighbour almost four miles away, the only sounds the bleating of sheep, the call of grouse and curlew and the wind keening across the moor.

Winter snows can cut off the Tan Hill Inn from the outside world for weeks at a time

The wind blows so strongly here that many incautious motorists have lost their car doors to it – one famous landlady declared that it blew hard enough to 'blow the horns off a tup' (the local word for a ram) – and in winter it can whip the snow up into huge drifts that block the inn off from the outside world for weeks at a time.

A tale is told of the landlord who wished a shepherd 'Happy New Year' on 16 April because he was the first person he had seen that year. In another winter it was so cold that the whisky froze in the optics behind the bar! The Swaledale breed of sheep, with their distinctive black faces and white noses, was developed in the area around Tan Hill, and they are so hardy that they live up on 'the tops' in all but the wildest weather and can survive on a diet that would starve almost any other breed. If buried under the snow they have been known to survive for weeks, even eating their own fleeces to do so.

Tan Hill's isolation is lessened by the annual influx of summer tourists, and on the last Thursday in May every year it plays host to the Swaledale sheep world championships – the Tan Hill Show. On that day, a thousand people will be there to look at the sheep or just to share in the atmosphere of a unique event – there is no other country show like it. The judging of the sheep is deadly serious – a champion tup can command a price of well into five figures – and the judges' decisions will be discussed and disputed far into the night. The uninvolved can simply sit outside on a warm spring evening and listen as the sound of a silver band playing the local anthem 'Beautiful Swaledale' drifts over the fells.

Tan Hill is absolutely unique. See it in summer, surrounded by ten thousand acres of wild moorland. In winter snows it is best to leave it to the sheep and the shepherds who have learned to live with its wild weather – if you are lucky you may be stranded in the inn for some weeks and will have some tales to tell your friends; but if you are not so lucky, you may be dead from exposure before help can reach you.

Travel down from Tan Hill by the narrow, often precipitous roads that pass over the 'tops' separating each dale from the next, and you will begin to capture a little of the flavour and variety of the Yorkshire Dales. The first is Swaledale – the loveliest of them all – once home to scores of mines which supplied the lead that roofed the great cathedrals of France and the Norman castles of England. The ruins of the mines still remain, but the dale now exists on farming and tourism.

Swaledale sheep, so hardy that they can survive buried beneath the snow for weeks

For centuries the narrow steep-sided dale, with its waterfalls and fast-rushing river, was cut off from the outside world by the fells that surround it. Its inhabitants, descendants of the Norse who settled the area, grew up with their own special dialect and customs and with a complete disinterest in those not lucky enough to have been born in the 'beautiful dale'.

Farming was a back-breaking and often heart-breaking struggle for survival in a climate whose winter ferocity belies the gentle warmth of its summer days. Although the winters are no less severe, and farmers' incomes are small in comparison with those of their lowland cousins, the present-day sheep-farmers enjoy a standard of living that their forefathers could not have dreamed of.

Swaledale was the last dale to be 'discovered' by tourism, but the success of the James Herriot books, and the films and TV programmes shot in the area, has brought it a new crop – of tourists – who pause to marvel at the patchwork of dry-stone walls, field barns and beautiful villages nestling round the Swale. In spring and early summer you will be able to see wild flowers here that have all but disappeared from the rest of Britain, and the hay meadows are a mass of flowers and herbs that have grown undisturbed for close on a thousand years.

The Farmers Arms, Muker, as the name suggests, is a true farmers' local
Opposite: The idyllic setting of the White Lion at Cray

In the heart of Upper Swaledale you will find the lovely village of Muker, with its unpretentious local, the Farmers Arms, set back from the road. Once undisturbed by more than a few visitors, Muker takes its increasing popularity in its stride. It's a perfect starting-point for a walk up the Swale along the flanks of Kisdon – the hill dominating the village.

Part of the way you'll be travelling along the Corpse Way, an ancient footpath once used to bring the dead from the upper dale down to their last resting-place in 'the cathedral of the dales' – the church at Grinton – which was the nearest consecrated ground before the church at Muker was built. The dead were carried on men's shoulders, and there still remain a few of the large, flat stone slabs by the side of the path on which they would rest their burden.

Walk along one side of the river to the waterfalls beyond Keld; if it's hot you can cool off with a swim in one of the deep pools full of darting brown trout. Then you can return along the other side in time for a drink and a bite to eat at the Farmers Arms. You can sit out on the terrace at the front or in the single, L-shaped room inside, which has a carpeted area at one end and huge stone flags and an open fire at the other. It's as warmly welcoming a pub as you could wish to find and, despite its popularity with visitors, it retains its local character. Even in the depths of winter, when the last tourist has gone home, the Farmers Arms remains a thriving centre of village life.

Cross into Wensleydale by the Buttertubs Pass (named after a series of deep holes in the ground) and you'll have the chance of a small detour to Hardraw Force – the highest single drop waterfall in England – approached through the Green Dragon pub. The Force is in a huge natural amphitheatre which has been used for brass band concerts since the nineteenth century. The best time to see Hardraw is after heavy rain, when the sight and sound of the Force crashing into the pool at the bottom of its long drop will send shivers down your spine.

Wensleydale is entirely different from Swaledale, but as beautiful in its own way – a broad, U-shaped valley which is unique in the dales for not being named after the river, the Ure, that flows through it. There is also one of the few lakes in the dales, Semerwater, which arose, so local legend goes, to engulf a village where a mysterious stranger was refused food and shelter. Such a fate is unlikely

The Farmers Arms
Licensees: William & Elsie Whitehead
Muker, nr Richmond, North Yorkshire
☎ Richmond (0748) 86297
11-3; 6-11

Theakston XB

Lunchtime & evening food. Bunkhouse accommodation. Families welcome. Camping available nearby.

to befall you at any of the Dale's many excellent pubs, unless you fall foul of our antiquated licensing laws.

When you reach Askrigg, call at the Crown in the Main Street, which retains its traditional Dales character despite modernisation. After exploring Wensleydale to your heart's content, leave through the bustling market town of Hawes, before climing up a seemingly endless steep hill towards Fleet Moss and Cam Fell. You pass Wether Fell, from where hang-gliders launch themselves, and you cross an old Roman road. On the tops here are marvellous views of the Yorkshire hills, including Ingleborough – not the highest Yorkshire mountain, but by far the most imposing.

You will now descend through the lovely village of Oughtershaw and through Langstrothdale, where the river splashes among rocks beside the road. Turn left in Hubberholme, where there is a twelfth-century church and a very pleasant pub, the George, and keep to the left, travelling up towards the very head of Wharfedale to the White Lion at Cray.

It's an old pack-horse traders' and drovers' inn, with a single, stone-flagged bar, a big open fireplace and a warm and welcoming atmosphere. It's unpretentious but very friendly, and, unlike many pubs in tourist areas, it remains unspoilt – very much a pub, not a tourist curiosity or a restaurant masquerading as a pub.

There is a lovely little garden to sit in when the weather is fine, set above the narrow road that leads back over into Wensleydale, but best of all is to sit by the stream across the road on a warm summer's evening, watching the swallows skimming over the surface of the water and listening to the liquid call of the curlew up on the fells.

When you are rested and refreshed enough, drop back down Wharfedale through Buckden, Starbotton and Kettlewell and turn off towards Arncliffe just before you reach Kilnsey Crag, a limestone face much used by rock climbers. The Falcon in Arncliffe is another delightfully unspoilt pub in another lovely village, but our route takes us out of Littondale, over towards Malham. The area around Malham Tarn is a haven for rare plants and you should not miss Malham Cove, one of the great sights of the dales, a massive limestone cliff over which a river once tumbled in a waterfall to rival Niagara. The cove remains a spectacular

The White Lion
Licensee: Linda Emmott
Cray, nr Buckden, North Yorkshire
☎ Kettlewell (075 676) 262
11-3; 5.30-10.30
(11 Friday, Saturday & summer)

Goose Eye Bitter; Younger Scotch Bitter; Guest beers

Lunchtime & evening food. Garden. Families welcome.

The Game Cock Inn, at the heart of Austwick village

place, though the river has long since found another course, disappearing underground, like so many in this limestone country, to carve out a network of potholes and caverns which draws thousands of cavers to the dales every year.

From Malham take either of the roads leading west and make your way beyond Settle to Austwick, just off the main A65, where you will find the Game Cock. You are safely away from the traffic rumbling through to the Lake District on the main road a mile away, and from the seats outside the pub you can enjoy the peace and quiet of this pretty village.

Inside you will find a small bar, plainly furnished, but polished till it gleams. It is popular with visitors by day and locals by night, and you will be certain of a warm welcome and friendly service. There is a small dining-room, and the inn also has accommodation. The Game Cock makes an excellent base from which to explore the Three Peaks, Ingleborough, Whernside and Pen-y-ghent. If you feel fit enough, try and walk the three of them in one day and spare a thought for the competitors in the annual Three Peaks Race, who have to run!

You are also within easy reach of the most spectacular part of the Settle–Carlisle railway line, the viaduct at Ribblehead. Built during the Victorian railway boom, the line proved a hazardous venture, crossing some of the wildest and least hospitable country in England. The cost in money and human life was

The Game Cock
Licensee: Mary Howarth
Austwick, nr Skipton, North Yorkshire
☎ Clapham (046 85) 226
11-3; 5.30-10.30
(11 Friday, Saturday & summer)

Thwaites Bitter

Lunchtime & evening food. Accommodation. Families welcome. Outdoor drinking area.

massive, particularly during the building of the Ribblehead Viaduct.

Millions of tons of stone disappeared into the peat bogs of Blea Moor, and hundreds died in the tented villages that sprang up to house the army of navvies building the line. The dead lie buried in the churchyard at the lovely little church of St Leonard in Chapel-le-Dale, with a stone plaque on the church wall as their monument. The Settle–Carlisle line is under threat of closure, so, if you have the time, take the opportunity to travel on it, for it is one of the world's great railway journeys and a fine way to see the heads of the Western Dales.

One of the three bridges across Linton Beck leading to the Fountaine Inn

To reach the last classic pub of the dales, either travel back past Malham or head towards Skipton and turn left on to the Grassington road. Turn off to the right immediately after a remarkably ugly limestone works and you'll reach the remarkably beautiful village of Linton-in-Craven. A small monument was erected on the village green to commemorate Linton being adjudged to be the prettiest village in the North in a 1949 newspaper competition, and it is hard to fault the judges' choice. Linton Beck meanders through the village green, crossed by a ford and a narrow pack-horse bridge, built in the fourteenth century.

At the south end of the green is an even older bridge, the 'clapper' bridge, and the Fountaine Hospital Chapel and Almshouses. Hospital is here used in its original sense of refuge, and the building is alleged to have been designed by Vanbrugh, architect of Castle Howard and Blenheim Palace, which we passed some time and many pubs ago. Richard Fountaine, a native of Linton, made a fortune from timber in London at the time of the Plague, selling coffins for the dead, so it is claimed. At his own death, he bequeathed money to build an almshouse for 'six poor men or women' of the parish. The houses are still lived in and the chapel is still in use. The building is named after Richard Fountaine, as is the village pub, the Fountaine Inn.

Inside you will find a small, cosy bar and a snug with a curved pine-boarded settle, a fine stone fireplace and the ancient pub game of Ring the Bull. Up a couple of steps there is a light, airy extension with comfortable seats, but if you have children with you, most interest will be focused on the children's room, the 'Lion's Den'. The reason for the name will be obvious as soon as you step through the door; the small room is dominated by a snarling stuffed lion! It is guaranteed to keep children amused for hours, giving you a chance to enjoy the character, atmosphere and good company of a fine English pub.

Most Wharfedale tourists go to Grassington, and for that reason I would miss it out and instead follow the Wharfe down through the pretty villages of Burnsall and Appletreewick – both, inevitably, with lovely pubs – to Bolton Abbey, part of the estates of the Dukes of Devonshire, where you can walk along the river by the ruins of Bolton Priory. There is a nature trail through Strid Wood, where the Wharfe is compressed into a narrow, treacherous torrent. In Victorian times, young men used to prove their virility by jumping over the Strid; do not be tempted to emulate them. If you fall in the water, you will be swept away; many people have drowned there.

On summer weekends, like much of Wharfedale, Bolton Abbey is heaving with people. On this trip it will be your last impression of the dales, so try to visit it early or late in the day, or else in spring or autumn, when you may have it rather more to yourself. Then follow the Wharfe down through Ilkey, Otley and Pool, and it will lead you past Harewood House, a very stately home, with some justly famous bird gardens that you may wish to see.

Follow the Wharfe valley beyond Harewood towards Collingham, then turn south through the village of East Keswick to Bardsey, home of another country

The 'Lion's Den' at the Fountaine Inn at Linton-in-Craven, guaranteed to keep the children quiet!

The Fountaine Inn
Licensees: David & Pat Clark
Linton-in-Craven, nr Skipton, North Yorkshire
☎ Grassington (0756) 752210
11.30-3; 6.30-10.30
(11 Friday, Saturday & summer)

Taylor Best Bitter, Landlord; Tetley Bitter; Theakston Best Bitter, Old Peculier

Lunchtime & evening food. Families welcome. Outdoor drinking area.

classic, perhaps the genuine holder of the title of England's oldest inn. The Bingley Arms at Bardsey, originally known as the Priests Inn, is mentioned in 'Domesday Book' and actually dates back to AD 953. A brewhouse stood alongside the inn for a thousand years and members of the same family ran it from the time of Samson Ellis, the first recorded keeper, until 1780. It was at that time that Baron Bingley changed the name of the pub.

The central part of the pub is the original building, and the later extensions and the original roofline can be clearly seen. The ceilings were raised in the seventeenth century from the original height of five feet eleven inches. The inn was used as a rest house for monks travelling to St Mary's at York from Kirkstall Abbey until the Dissolution of the Monasteries; after that it found secular use as a coaching inn.

The lounge bar contains a massive stone ingle-nook; step into the fireplace and look upwards and you will see a 'priest's hole'. The North of England was the heartland of loyalty to the 'old religion' in the time of the Tudors, and many old houses had such a hiding-place, where a catholic priest or one of his flock who had expressed his religious convictions incautiously could be hidden from the King's men.

There is a small, wood-panelled dining-room off the lounge, and at the other end of the inn is the Dutch Oven Room – so named, unsurprisingly, for the Dutch oven it contains, dating from 1738 and still in its original position. At the rear of the building are a series of narrow, terraced lawns with wooden tables where you can sit in summer and enjoy the flowers. The top floor of the building, containing a restaurant, is dominated by the vast stone chimney-breast of the ingle-nook below, and in the walls you can see the ring trusses and beam holes of the original roof.

The Bingley Arms is steeped in a thousand years of history; it is a shame that some of the beauty and character of the building is devalued by the kitsch treatment of its interior. 'Wenches' and 'Swains' on the doors to the lavatories are bad enough; even worse is the use of décor that would look out of place in a 1930s Hollywood costume drama, and the most obvious fake adzed beams. If it had to be faked, it seems a pity not to have faked it with genuine old materials instead of twentieth-century tat.

Despite all this, the Bingley Arms remains a classic pub, because of its antiquity and its character, but only just. Many other once fine pubs have suffered an even more

The Bingley Arms
Bardsey, nr Leeds, West Yorkshire
☎ Collingham Bridge (0937) 72462
11-3; 6-10.30
(11 Thursday, Friday & Saturday)

Tetley Mild, Bitter

Lunchtime & evening food. Restaurant Tuesday to Saturday evening and Sunday lunch. Garden. Families welcome.

An unusual, stained glass window at the Bingley Arms, Bardsey

hideous fate at the hands of insensitive designers and developers. At the Bingley Arms you are on the borderline; I suggest you drink a toast to those classic pubs that survive, and another in memory of those that have disappeared.

You may also like to raise your glass to the English dramatist William Congreve, born in Bardsey in 1670 and most remembered for the lines:

Music has charms to soothe a savage breast.
Heaven has no rage like love to hatred turned,
Nor Hell a fury like a woman scorned.

Before you leave Bardsey, take a few minutes to look at the other ancient building in the village, the church. Its Saxon tower is in perfect condition and is probably one of the finest in Europe.

Our road now takes us into one of the most heavily industrialised areas of Yorkshire, but one containing an 'oasis' where you will find another classic country pub. Take the A58 in towards Leeds, then follow the ring road south to the A63 to Selby. Turn right at the crossroads with the A656 towards Castleford and take the small road to the left that leads you down to Ledsham.

This part of Yorkshire is the borderland between the high country of the Pennines and the flatlands of the Yorkshire grain prairies that sweep from here to the North Sea. It is also the heart of the Yorkshire coalfield, and the nearest pit heap and power station are never far away.

The surrounding industrialisation makes the village of Ledsham all the more surprising, for it is a lovely village, of stone houses, church and pub, that could be in the heart of rural England instead of a stone's throw from the Yorkshire coalfield. The Chequers is an ivy- and creeper-covered pub at the heart of the village. On entering you pass under an arch into a yard with a raised terrace where you can sit and enjoy a quiet drink on a warm evening.

The Chequers at Ledsham, a rural pub, but surrounded by a Yorkshire coalfield

Inside the Chequers is a central bar, serving four delightful small rooms. Three of them have blazing open fires to keep out the winter cold, and the pub atmosphere is as warm and welcoming as a fireside on a frosty morning. Though the Chequers is considerably less ancient than the Bingley Arms, it has a great deal more atmosphere and much more of the feeling of a Great British pub than its more venerable rival.

The Chequers has a restaurant upstairs, but it does not dominate the pub trade in the way that many do; at the Chequers the restaurant is a pleasant addition to the range of good reasons for going there, not the only one. The pub does have one small fault, however. Visit it on a Sunday and you will think you have inadvertently strayed back into one of the barren, arid regions of Wales; the Chequers is closed on Sunday.

The Chequers
Licensee: George Wraith
Claypit Lane, Ledsham, nr Castleford, West Yorkshire
☎ South Milford (0977) 683135
11-3; 5.30-10.30
(11 Thursday, Friday & Saturday). Closed Sunday

Theakston Best Bitter, XB; Younger Scotch Bitter, No. 3

Lunchtime & evening food. Restaurant Tuesday to Saturday. Garden. Families welcome.

To the Peak District and the Midlands

'They faced the amphitheatre of round hills that flowed with sunset, tiny white farms standing out, the meadows golden, the woods dark and yet luminous, tree-tops folded over tree-tops, distinct in the distance. The evening had cleared, and the east was tender with a magenta flush under which the land lay still and rich.'

SONS AND LOVERS
D H LAWRENCE

The 'dark satanic mills' that once stretched across industrial Yorkshire and Lancashire are now largely silent. The dirt and squalor have been greatly cleaned up, but with the grime have gone most of the jobs that the mills provided. 'From Hull and Hell and Halifax, Good Lord deliver me' was a plea for rescue from the appalling conditions of Victorian industrial towns; now it is more likely to be the prayer of Rugby League supporters waiting for the draw for the first round of the Challenge Cup. With the decline of the North, much of the character and a great deal of the architectural heritage of its cities has been lost, but there is still much to savour on the way south to the Peak District and the next country classic pub.

Leave Ledsham by the road to Ferrybridge and have the bucolic idyll demolished instantaneously by the sight of the huge cooling towers of the Ferrybridge power station. After turning west on the M62 you will pass through the heart of the Yorkshire coalfield. Pontefract grew rich on two kinds of 'black gold'; the coal, and the liquorice that is made into 'Pontefract cakes'. The West Riding 'capital' of Leeds; the wool city, Bradford; Halifax with its superb Piece Hall; Haworth with its Brontë connections and its steam railway; Huddersfield, the home of the best choral singing this side of Wales: all are worth seeing, but make your way steadily towards Sheffield, the city where cutlery is still king, even if the steel industry is no longer the dominant force it once was. The industrial area sprawls to the east of the city centre; our road lies to the west.

Sheffield is left behind with a suddenness which is startling for such a large city. One minute you are ploughing through the suburbs, the next you are out and heading into the High Peak. We last encountered the Pennine Way high on Tan Hill, one hundred miles to the north; now we are travelling to its starting point, Edale, to visit the Old Nags Head.

The Pennine Way is a 270-mile trudge along the 'backbone of England'. Most people who walk it do so from south to north, and there must be a few who have sat at the stone tables outside the Nags Head, looking up at the dark, brooding mass of Kinder Scout, the first peak on the Way, thought about the miles of glutinous peat bog and gruelling peat hags beyond, and decided to take a motoring holiday instead.

The pub is a pleasant old stone building,

The Old Nags Head
Licensee: Denis Liston
Edale, Derbyshire
☎ Hope Valley (0433) 70212
11-3; 6-11 (winter 12-2.30; 7-11)

Marston Pedigree; Younger Scotch Bitter

Lunchtime & evening food. Families welcome. Garden.

The Old Nags Head at Edale, the point of no return for walkers on the Pennine Way

not too spoilt by its 'Brewers' Tudor' half-timbered bays. There is a comfortable lounge with a huge stone fireplace dominated by a stag's head, and, of course, a hikers' bar where the Pennine Wayfarers and those with less ambitious walking plans can compare experiences and discuss routes. There is also a family room, and, when the Pennine weather relents, you can sit at the stone seats and tables outside. The village peace in this quiet and remote valley is only disturbed by the regular tramp of hiking boots and by a flood of summer visitors.

From Edale, make your way round either westwards under the shadow of Mam Tor, if the road is not blocked by a landslide, or eastwards to Hope. In either case, stop at Castleton for a look at Peveril Castle, a ruin dramatically poised on a cliff-top at the head of a steep, rocky gorge. Nearby are the Bluejohn Caverns where you can explore the workings and buy pieces of this strange Derbyshire fluorspar.

Take the minor road that goes due south out of Castleton towards Little Hucklow. This road shows you the vast scale of mineral extraction in the Peaks. There is a massive working quarry in the bottom of the valley, and rising up towards the summit are progressively older workings, the earliest partly re-conquered by nature, as the scars of mining have been softened by erosion and the spread of vegetation.

The bleak grandeur of the High Peak is

The Old Bulls Head
Licensee: D. G. Hawketts
Little Hucklow, Derbyshire
☎ Tideswell (0298) 871097
12-3 (closed winter weekdays); 5.30-11

Winkle Ivanhoe, Saxon Cross

Food: snacks only. Garden.

now exchanged for the gentler, rolling foot-hills of the Pennines. At Little Hucklow, just off the B6049, north of the A623 between Chapel-en-le-Frith and Chesterfield, you will find a pretty village nestling around a meandering country lane. At the bottom of the village is the Old Bulls Head. The first thing you will notice, if you are travelling in summer, is the riot of colour from the flowers which throng the gardens, and sprout from tubs everywhere you look.

The second thing to catch your eye will probably be the pub's vast collection of 'bygones'. Agricultural implements from the past, painted black, are scattered around the

The Old Bulls Head at Little Hucklow, surrounded by a colourful garden in summer Opposite: The unusual sign of the Chequers at Froggatt Edge

land surrounding the pub and festoon the whitewashed walls as well. Hames, picks, shovels and nameless implements dangle from chains around the walls, and on top of the porch there is an old plough as well as a pair of flower tubs. Beyond the car-park are two enormous millstones and an old horse-drawn plough; there are a couple of stone cheese-presses, and cartwheels everywhere.

Inside the pub, the 'bygone' theme is continued with a collection of old household utensils, locally mined geological specimens and a collection of African carvings for good measure. There are two small oak-beamed rooms, one with a serving hatch, and in winter there is an open fire blazing in the stone fireplace. Food is limited to snacks like ploughman's lunches and sandwiches, and the pub does not open on weekday lunchtimes in winter. If trade is slack, the landlord may

close early at other times, so if you are travelling some distance, it may pay to telephone ahead.

From Little Hucklow you can either travel across country by the minor roads or drop down on to the main A623 and turn east towards the next Peak District classic pub, the Chequers at Froggatt Edge, above the valley of the River Derwent. These steeply wooded valleys and fast rivers of the Peaks were among the birthplaces of the Industrial Revolution in Britain, where manufacturers began to make use of the water power available to drive their new machines. The area is rich in industrial archaeological remains, though most of the industry has long departed.

To reach the Chequers, turn north at the junction with the B6001 and keep to the right on to the B6054, climbing towards the steep rocky scarp that gives Froggatt Edge its name, after passing a river where you can fish at the bottom of the hill. The Chequers sits by the side of the steep hill climbing towards Shef-field. It was once four separate houses but is now one long building. Honeysuckle and roses ramble across its walls; there are flower tubs outside and geraniums in pots along the window sills. Across the road is a car-park as long and narrow as the pub itself, and beyond it a steep slope drops away into a wooded valley.

The Chequers is a typically English pub. Though it serves excellent bar and restaurant food, this has not been allowed to overwhelm its role as a pub, and it enjoys a thriving local trade. It has blazing open fires and a family room and makes a fine place to break your journey and spend the night, before leaving the Peaks for the journey south through the Midlands.

At Froggatt Edge you are close to Chatsworth House, the seat of the Dukes of Devonshire, and a magnificent stately home with superb grounds and water gardens. Follow the Derwent south beyond Baslow to reach it. Before travelling on to the next country classic, you might also want to make a detour east to Chesterfield to look at the cathedral with the famous crooked spire. Some fault in its construction caused the spire to corskcrew around on itself, and although this twisted spire is perfectly safe, it looks likely to complete the circle and fall off at any moment!

Head south from Froggatt Edge, picking up the A6 past Haddon Hall, a twelfth-

The Chequers
Licensees: Mr & Mrs McLeod
Froggatt Edge, nr Chesterfield, Derbyshire
☎ Hope Valley (0433) 30231
11-3; 5-30-11

Ward Sheffield Bitter

Lunchtime & evening food. Restaurant. Accommodation. Families welcome.

The Yew Tree
Licensee: D. East
Cauldon, Staffordshire
☎ Waterhouses (053 86) 348
10.30-2.30; 6-11

Draught Bass; Ind Coope Bitter; M & B Mild; Winkle Saxon Cross

Bar snacks at most times. Families welcome. Small garden.

century manor house, well worth visiting for its superb rose gardens. Turn west as you approach Matlock, actually one of five Matlocks spread down this beautiful part of the Derwent valley, and you will pass through the equally beautiful Dovedale, dropping down on to the A523. You will find our next stop, the village of Cauldon, just south of this road, midway between Leek and Ashbourne.

From the approach to the Yew Tree at Cauldon, you would never guess that you are about to walk into one of the finest pubs in the country. Two hundred yards one way is a quarry, and four hundred yards the other is a cement works. The pub's next-door neigh-

The Yew Tree at Cauldon boasts a remarkable collection of antiques

bour is an electricity sub-station.

The pub is as old as the yew tree outside, dating back to the late seventeenth century. The front bar is original, but other bits have been built on in piecemeal fashion over the years. When the Easts bought the Yew Tree twenty-five years ago, it was unfashionable to own a freehouse and country pubs were not as popular as they are today. Heavy, carved oak furnishings were looked on as junk, and Victorian music machines were a joke. So the Easts bought the lot.

The entrance is impressive. Whereas the average pub will warrant a quick look around, the Yew Tree demands a careful inspection. Before you reach the bar, you will have passed by several polyphonia and a symphonion, a small collection of grandfather clocks, a penny-farthing, an ancient rocking-horse and much more.

If you have your family with you, they will have to sit on the settees with the padding falling out, among the other music machines and opposite glass cases containing the antique beer collection. The lounge hides its penny-farthing behind the upright, padded, ornately carved settle. The flintlocks on the wall are less impressive than the pianola with its one hundred and fifty music rolls. Drinking at the bar, you will inevitably spot the Acme Patent Dog Carrier, a Victorian joke with a muzzle at one end and a conical screw at the other.

The front bar boasts table skittles and a remarkably modern-looking dartboard for those who do not simply wish to sit and sup at the central bar or chat to Mr East, his mum or his aunt about what they are collecting nowadays. The heavy-duty cash registers, gas masks, copper kettles, painted truncheons and serpents are just 'extras' to them. Nowadays they are collecting old black-and-white televisions and radiograms; all rubbish, of course.

In case you are still wondering, a polyphonion is a large standing musical box in an ornate casing which, for the sum of twopence, will play its tinkly tune for a couple of minutes. It is the only background music in the place, unless the Easts allow a concert on the pianola.

The Cauldon village well, dating from 1878, is inscribed, 'Thy clouds drop fatness'; nowadays, they also drop dust. Cauldon is a lovely village overshadowed by a vast mineral extraction plant. It is a perfect example of the conflict of interests, in areas of great landscape beauty, between the National Parks, who tend to put the landscape before everything, and the local people who love their surroundings but also want jobs.

Y ou will probably part company with Cauldon's pub with rather more regret than its cement works, but you will find the next classic in another lovely Peak District village, this time untarnished by the demands of the construction industry. Travel east through the delightful town of Ashbourne, which contains a traffic warning sign which must be unique: 'Swans Crossing', and turn north three miles further on.

Continuing up a winding road with hedgerows either side, at the top of a hill you'll find the village of Kirk Ireton. A solid Norman church stands at one end of the village; at the other is the Barley Mow. There's a sun-dial high on the front of the building, dating it to 1683, though the back

The Barley Mow
Licensee: Mary Short
Kirk Ireton, Derbyshire
12-2; 7-10.30

Draught Bass; Marston Pedigree; Theakston Bitter, Old Peculier

Lunchtime & evening food.

Opposite: The Barley Mow at Kirk Ireton, probably once the manor house, now a delightfully unspoilt pub

part is older still. It looks more like a manor house than a pub, and may once have been one, though it has been an inn for at least two hundred years.

Take a deep breath as you step through the door – you could almost be stepping back that many years. The Barley Mow is utterly unspoilt, a rambling collection of tile-floored, oak-beamed rooms, unaltered, except for the addition of electric light, since the turn of the century. The bar has very unusual slate-topped tables and a big open fireplace. The beer is stillaged on a stone shelf behind the bar and dispensed by gravity into enamel jugs. There is a tiny parlour with oak chairs and pews, and two other rooms, one doubling as the pub kitchen.

The Barley Mow is another of the many pubs that owes much of its character to an indomitable landlady, in this case a Mrs Ford who lived there throughout her eighty-nine years and ran the pub until she died. For the last few years of her life she was unable to walk, but she continued to preside over the bar from a seat by the fire and, though you ordered your drink from her staff, Mrs Ford collected the money personally!

The present licensee has been at the inn for over ten years and has kept it much as it was in Mrs Ford's time. Other major attractions of this excellent pub are a vast black Newfoundland dog called Chester and a one-eyed black cat.

The Crown at Old Dalby is a rarity, a pub that has added on a fine restaurant without losing any of its character

From Kirk Ireton our route runs south-east and you can choose between the twin East Midlands 'capitals' of Derby and Nottingham along the way. I prefer Nottingham and would travel through there. Cut through the Nottinghamshire coalfield, with its blackened industrial villages and ravaged landscapes, now greening as the slag heaps are covered with a cosmetic layer of grass. You will pass close to Eastwood, home territory of D. H. Lawrence and the setting for his novel *Sons and Lovers*.

Nottingham has suffered much the same ravages at the hands of the planners as our other great cities, but you should certainly visit the Lace Market, the castle, and, even more important, the Trip to Jerusalem. This is an ancient pub carved out of the rock on which the castle stands, named after the Crusaders who paused for refreshment on their way to the Holy Land. Nottingham Castle of course has links to everybody's favourite outlaw, Robin Hood, but the present building is a seventeenth-century mansion, now the City Museum. You can still

The Crown
Licensee: Lynne Bryan
Old Dalby, Leicestershire
☎ Melton Mowbray (0664) 823134
10-2.30; 6.30-11

Beer range varies, good selection from Hardys & Hansons; Hook Norton; Marston; Ruddle; Theakston

Lunchtime & evening food. Restaurant. Garden. Families welcome.

explore the catacombs in the Castle Rock, where, no doubt, the Sheriff of Nottingham imprisoned such outlaws as he could lay his hands on.

When you have seen enough of Nottingham, take the A606 towards Melton Mowbray, crossing the Fosse Way, now more prosaically known as the A46, and turn off in Nether Broughton to Old Dalby. The Crown at Old Dalby is a remarkable old pub, more like a private house, consisting of several small cottage rooms, with antique chairs and settles, open fires and hunting prints on the walls. Step into the pub through the back door and you are confronted by the large range of cask beers stillaged behind the serving hatch. The landlady, Lynne Bryan, maintains the Crown's tradition of always having had a woman licensee; her partner Salvatore Inguanta looks after the tiny restaurant, with its enticing menu.

This is a rare and unspoilt old Leicestershire pub, with a plain exterior untouched since the pub's days as a farmhouse. There is a pleasant terrace at the back and a large lawn, with trees and roses, where you can play *boules* or croquet.

When you leave Old Dalby, rejoin the main road and travel south through Melton Mowbray, home town of Stilton cheese and pork pies. Continue south, past Rutland Water, once in England's smallest county and now just a

The Falcon
Licensee: Alan Stewart
Fotheringhay,
Northamptonshire
☎ Cotterstock (08326) 342
11-2.30; 6-11

Elgoods EB; Greene King IPA; Liddington Bitter

Lunchtime & evening food (last orders 9.45). No food on Monday. Garden. Families welcome.

The Falcon at Fotheringhay is a fitting complement to a beautiful and historic village

memory, and head east on the A47. Turn off just before you reach the A1, and drive south through Yarwell and Nassington to Fotheringhay.

Fotheringhay has entered English and Scottish history as the place where the head of the indiscreet Mary Queen of Scots took its leave of the rest of her. As well as the remains of the twelfth-century castle where Mary was incarcerated and beheaded, the village has a particularly lovely church, which is floodlit at night, and a particularly fine pub.

Before the present landlord bought The Falcon, it was voted 'the grottiest pub in Northants' by the local young farmers. Twenty years of brewery neglect have since been remedied; it is now a freehouse and very far from grotty. The Falcon has a very small bar where the locals congregate and a lounge/restaurant where you can eat some excellent food at very reasonable prices. All the food is home-made and as traditional as you would expect, but all too rarely find, in a fine old English pub.

This is another nouvelle cuisine-free zone. Fill up on the traditional steak and kidney pie, or rabbit cooked in cider with apple and walnuts, with one of the home-made puddings to follow. Fotheringhay is a popular spot with tourists and day-trippers. If you arrive by car, drive carefully; if you are travelling by boat, you can park it near the Falcon, where moorings are available.

Southwick is another in the seemingly limitless number of beautiful villages in this part of England, with the fine fourteenth-century hall your first sight of it as you approach from the north. It may seem perverse to choose another pub not five miles from the Falcon, but the Shuckburgh Arms at Southwick is a different, but equally excellent pub, a true local.

The Shuckburgh Arms (I was assured by an entirely straight-faced landlord that the name Shuckburgh means 'a watering-hole for elves') is a sixteenth-century thatched building which was once the village bakehouse. Now its small bar and comfortable lounge are the focus of a thriving range of activities, from meetings of a folk club and charity events, to the village cricket matches played on the ground behind the pub.

If cricket is too strenuous for you, there is a bar-billiards table in the pub, and if even that seems mildly energetic, settle down in a deckchair and watch the cricket with a drink for company. Cricket on the green with the village pub close by is one of those timeless

Opposite: A quiet country lane and a quiet country pub; the Shuckburgh Arms at Southwick

The Shuckburgh Arms
Licensees: Tony & Jan Parsons
Main Street, Southwick, Northamptonshire
☎ Oundle (0832) 74007
11-2.30; 6-11

Adnams Bitter; Hook Norton Best Bitter; Ruddle County

Lunchtime & evening food. Garden.

pleasures, the thought of which sends far-distant expatriates misty-eyed with nostalgia. Have another drink and reflect on the thought that a nation that invents a game that can last for five days and still not produce a winner must have got something right.

From Southwick, meander your way gently east through Cotterstock and Tansor, cross the A605 and make your way by the narrow winding lanes that lead you to Stilton. The mile-long, pencil-straight high street used to be part of the Roman Ermine Street, running from London to Edinburgh. Its successor, the modern A1, the

The Bell Inn
Licensees: M. J. McGivern & L. A. McGivern
Stilton, Cambridgeshire
☎ Peterborough (0733) 241066
11-2.30; 6-11

Marston Pedigree; Ruddle County; Tetley Bitter

Bar meals lunchtime & evening. Restaurant Wednesday & Saturday. Garden.

The hefty, wrought-iron inn sign of the Bell Inn at Stilton dominates the street

frantic, lorry-laden Great North Road, now skirts the village, which provides a pleasant refuge.

The Bell Inn is a seventeenth-century coaching inn of the grand sort. Solidly built in stone, it has a sign overhanging the wide pavement like an ornate exercise in Victorian mechanical engineering. When the bypass was built, it was feared that the village inns would wither and die, but happily the word is spreading that fine fare is to be had.

Stilton cheese is named after the village, but surprisingly it has never been produced there: it is made in Leicestershire. You would now know that from the Bell's menu, how-ever. If you feel the need, you can follow your delicious home-made Stilton soup with a variety of main dishes cooked with the cheese. Apparently the most traditional way to enjoy it is in thin slabs accompanied by plum bread.

The restaurant upstairs is impressively beamed, whilst the downstairs rooms feature stone walls and simple wood furnishings. Of course there is a large open fire, and the atmosphere, apart from the background muzak, approaches the baronial. The garden and patio areas at the back are spacious and neatly arranged.

To the Fens,
the Broads and
Constable Country

*'And no one needs telling that the land in that part
of the world is flat. Flat, with an unrelieved and
monotonous flatness, enough of itself, some might
say, to drive a man to unquiet and sleep-defeating
thoughts.'*

WATERLAND
GRAHAM SWIFT

'Very flat, Norfolk,' a character in Noel Coward's *Private Lives* said. People who have not been to East Anglia mistake flat for boring, but while the region may lack hills and rolling dales, it has its own distinctive character, a ruminative charm, and, in the remoter areas, a delightful sing-song dialect that is as difficult to mimic as it is to understand.

The East of England is one of the great cereal-producing regions of the country, and the reliance on the land for a living means that many areas are low in population. It is hard to believe that you are just a short drive from London as you negotiate narrow country lanes and come across small villages with weatherboarded cottages and thatched roofs, each village proudly displaying its distinctive cross or sign.

The coastal areas are as important as the rural ones for the wealth of the region. East Anglia is the gateway to Northern Europe, with docks, harbours and industrial areas in Lowestoft, Harwich, Felixstowe and Grimsby. In between, there are marshes, bird sanctuaries and miles of gritty, windy beaches with awesome views of sea and land stretching to the lowering horizon.

Batemans Wainfleet Brewery, with its windmill tower

The coastal area is dotted with many delightful and attractive small towns and villages, of which Aldeburgh and Southwold are the best known; the former for its association with Benjamin Britten (the Snape Maltings Concert Hall is nearby), the latter for its unspoilt Victorian charm and Adnam's seaside brewery.

The flatness of the region means that the great towns and cities do not leap up at you, but hover tantalisingly on the road ahead. The proud spires of Ely and Lincoln beckon from miles away. Cambridge and Norwich may be somewhat lost in their new urban sprawls. Yet, at their centres, the capitals of Cambridgeshire and Norfolk retain enormous charm and character: Cambridge, with the lawns of the great colleges running down to the river; Norwich, with its cobbled streets and the squat, doughty castle that looks protectively towards the cathedral.

Opposite: The tranquil waterside setting of the Locks at Geldeston

To reach these East Anglian delights leave Stilton to the south, joining the dual carriageway of the A1, perhaps the most difficult driving manoeuvre of the whole tour of Britain. The best route to the next classic pub lies across the heart of the Fens. One mile further south turn off the A1 on to the B660 and head to Ramsey, then north to Whittlesey and Thorney. This is old

The Four Horseshoes at South Eau Bank, Throckenholt, a basic pub but with excellent bitter

Huntingdonshire, where the Fenmen used to journey on stilts across the undrained marshes and the flats. Then came the agricultural engineers and reclaimed the land from the encroaching North Sea. You will see the orderly canals, 'the drains', as they are called, and the long, straight earthworks at their edges, 'the dykes'.

From Thorney, it is easiest to take the A47 Wisbech road and, shortly before Guyhirn, turn on to the B1187. Go past Parsons Drove and if you are careful you should spot the Four Horseshoes on your right. It is easily missed. In a hollow, it may well be below sea level, like much of the surrounding Fen. There are no fairy lights or neon brewery signs, no plush restaurant, no 'Brewer's Tudor' façade. There is not even a blazing log fire; for this is the archetypal basic Fenland boozer.

The excellent bitter has to be fetched from the back room, and the plain single bar offers only three amenities: darts, dominoes and conversation. They are used to strangers; for all the glitter and razzamatazz of modern country pubs, the Horseshoes attracts its customers by staying unfrilled.

Before sampling the pleasures of the Norfolk Broads, there is one more Fenland classic pub to be visited. Make your way north to Holbeach and follow the edge of the Wash to Boston. Granted a charter by King John in 1204, Boston was for a time the second biggest seaport in Britain, thriving on the wool trade with Flanders. Its

The Four Horseshoes
Licensee: Sylvia Delaney
South Eau Bank,
Throckenholt, nr Wisbech,
Lincolnshire
☎ Wisbech (0945) 700220
11-2; 7-11

Elgoods Bitter

heyday was in the thirteenth and fourteenth centuries, but its docks still bustle with activity. Its fourteenth-century church tower, known as 'the Stump', is a fen landmark for miles, the one highpoint in an ocean of flatlands. The Guildhall contains the cells in which some of the Pilgrim Fathers were incarcerated, before they sailed across the Atlantic and founded another Boston in the New World.

Take the A16 north from Boston and turn right on to the A158 towards 'so bracing' Skegness. For over one hundred years, holidaymakers from Nottingham, Mansfield, Leicester and the surrounding area have been travelling to Skegness. It is a sort of East Midlands Riviera, barely known by Southerners or folk from the real North.

Turning north towards Skendleby, you will come to the Blacksmiths Arms, run by Mrs Binch for half a lifetime. When she took it over with her late husband, they modernised it. There was no bar counter, so Mr Binch had to make one from the remains of an old wardrobe. The single bar measures little more than the average front room. It used to be smaller, but the high-backed settle has gone from one side of the fire; 'You could not get in through the front door', explained Mrs Binch. The fireplace dominates; a beautiful cast-iron, lamp-black monstrosity, adorned with brass and copper curios that shine like baubles on a Christmas tree.

Mrs Binch says that she will retire next year and that the future of the pub will depend on Batemans Brewery, known for

The Blacksmiths Arms
Licensee: Mrs Sarah Binch
Spilsby Road, Skendleby, nr Spilsby, Lincolnshire
10.30-2.30; 6-11

Batemans Bitter

The Blacksmiths Arms at Skendleby, one of Batemans Brewery's country taverns

their benevolent attitude towards their country taverns; but she has threatened to retire every year since 1978, so you never know. I told her that I would include her wonderful pub in this book anyway. She said that she did not want strangers coming on Friday lunchtimes. Why not? She always has her hair in curlers. You have been warned.

This part of Lincolnshire on a sunny summer day is a surprising panorama of rolling countryside. The temptation to drive through it to the ancient city of Lincoln, before turning south to the Broads, may be too strong to resist. The county town

An old smugglers' inn, the Lifeboat at Thornham Opposite: The delightful Kings Head at Laxfield

rises like an inland Mont St Michel from the surrounding land, peaked by its marvellous cathedral. Lincoln is built on the site of the Roman Lindum, at the intersection of two great highways, the Fosse Way and Ermine Street. As well as its cathedral, it has a twelfth-century Jewish quarter, a Guildhall, perched above the sixteenth-century town gate, and a wealth of fine medieval buildings. After exploring the city, turn to the south to begin the last lap of the journey, through the Norfolk Broads and Constable Country.

After taking the road down through Sleaford, you follow the A17 south-east to King's Lynn, a great fourteenth-century port, which, like Boston across the Wash, is now living very much on former glories. It is not the world's most handsome town, but the seventeenth-century Custom House on the quays is well worth visiting. Just

beyond King's Lynn is Castle Rising, which was a port when Lynn was just a marsh, and is the site of a fine Norman castle, surrounded by huge Roman earthworks. Castle Rising was one of the 'rotten boroughs' until the Reform Bill, and Horace Walpole and Samuel Pepys both sat for it.

Follow the coast road up through the charming seaside resort of Hunstanton, and on to Thornham. Turn off the main road at the King's Head, take the first left and you will find the delightful old inn, the Lifeboat, overlooking the marshes where the smugglers landed their contraband in centuries past. The Lifeboat is lit by oil lamps and has a lovely snug atmosphere at night, when the wind and rain come howling in across the flats. There are oak tables and oak panelling, five open fires in winter, low settles, tiled floors and beams hung with old reedcutters' tools. As well as shove ha'penny, dominoes and cribbage, there is a penny-in-the-hole bench.

At the back of the pub is a terraced area leading to a courtyard with seats under the trees. Across the road, doves coo in a 'dovecot' fashioned from an old beer cask in a tree. This warm, welcoming, unspoilt old inn offers limited accommodation and has a renowned restaurant, serving freshly caught sea-food.

Just south of Thornham you can pick up the Peddars Way, an ancient green way much older than the Roman road that used its line. It stretches from the Suffolk border to the Norfolk coast, where the Roman fort of Brancaster guarded the approaches to the Wash. Further along the coast are the great sweep of sands at Holkham, the charm of Brancaster Staithe, the seaside towns of Cromer, Sheringham, Blakeney and Wells, and the steam railway between Sheringham and Holt. Enjoy the beauty of this fine coast, then turn south towards Norwich.

Norwich city centre is contained in the square formed by the river and the old city walls. In medieval times Norwich was one of the richest cities in England, and, if its importance as a commercial centre faded as the Industrial Revolution concentrated the cloth trade in the North, it remains the principal city of East Anglia, and a place of great character and interest.

When you have seen your fill of the city, take the A146 south-east, turning east on to the A143 just before Beccles. Turn left at the sign to Geldeston, and keep going until you

The Lifeboat
Licensee: Nicholas Handley
Sea Lane, Thornham, Norfolk
☎ Thornham (048 526) 236
10.30-2.30; 6-11

Adnam Bitter, Old; Greene King XX, IPA, Abbot; Tolly Cobbold Bitter, Original

Bar snacks lunchtime & evening. Restaurant. Garden.

The Locks
Licensee: Mr G. N Harrison
Geldeston, Norfolk
☎ Kirby Cane (050 845) 414
10.30-2.30; 6-11 (closed weekdays in winter)

Adnam Bitter; Greene King IPA, Abbot

Lunchtime & evening food. Families welcome. Garden.

Not all of the customers at the Locks at Geldeston arrive by road

see a noticeboard pointing to the locks. The road peters out and becomes a bumpy track leading down to the River Waveney, which marks the boundary between Norfolk and Suffolk. At the riverside you will find a small, low-slung, one-bar pub, the Locks.

It was built in 1563 on the site of a windmill and was 'modernised' in 1666. The bar has a beamed ceiling and a large open fire, and locals will point to the spot above the fire marking the water level when the ravaging floods of 1953 poured into the pub and left it several feet under water.

The Locks is plain, unspoilt and hard to find, unless you go by boat. It is busy at weekends, and is popular with holidaymakers on the river, who can tie up and enjoy a drink either in the bar or on the spacious lawn leading down to the water. Campers often pitch their tents on the grass. The pub is closed on weekdays during the darkest days of winter, from New Year until Easter.

To reach the next classic pub, either drift south-west through the maze of minor roads across this sparsely popu-lated land, or follow the course of the Waveney west towards its source, and turn south on to the B1116 at Harleston. The road follows the line of a Roman road from Weybread to Fressingfield; a few miles further on it crosses the B1117, and a left turn will take you to Laxfield.

The term 'unspoilt' is applied to a good

many pubs nowadays which have escaped the brewers' last three rounds of renovations. It is rare to come across a pub which is in literally original condition. However, Laxfield's 'Low House', officially known as the Kings Head, is such a pub.

When the Parsons took over in 1982, its future had been in the balance. Adnam's brewery had sold it in 1972 because they were not sure it could ever be a going concern. The pub remained unaltered but few thought it could ever pay its way. The village is like many in rural East Suffolk and has a larger pub on the High Street which must gather much of the passing trade. Tucked behind the

Kings Head (Low House)
Licensee: Janet Parsons
Gorams Mill Lane,
Laxfield, Suffolk
☎ Ubbeston (098 683) 395
10.30-2.30; 6-11

Adnam Bitter, Extra;
Mauldons Bitter (in winter)

Lunchtime & evening food. Families welcome until 9 p.m. Garden.

The perfect end to a day's sailing, the Butt & Oyster at Pin Mill

cemetery, however, in the last place you would ever expect to find a pub, lies this gem of a place.

In the main room is a three-sided, high-backed settle arranged around an open fire. The area outside the settle has wall seating and a passageway. There is no bar, but on the way from the main room to the stillage room there is a parlour with a single table, suitable for playing cards, planning revolution or discussing the weather. The third, tiny room at the front makes for variety and demonstrates the merits of retaining small, cosy drinking spaces.

The beer is straight from the barrel, even in the outhouse, a loosely converted stables used only when summer trade demands an overspill area. The food is authentic. There are kippers, home-made soups, goats' milk cheeses and all manner of fanciful pies. The locally produced mustard is a masterpiece.

Outside is a bowling green and, with a bit of luck, croquet facilities should be coming soon. At present it is 'bring your own mallet', but they are working at that one. The formula for the pub is that if it remains unchanged then people will keep coming, but if it is modernised then it will fail. Appropriately it was the first ever outlet for James White's local ciders.

An eastward detour from Laxfield on to the A1120 Yoxford road will take you into real Adnam's country. It is well worth visiting Southwold, home of both the

A thatched gem in deepest Suffolk, the Cock at Brent Eleigh

famous brew and David Copperfield, to see the East Anglian coast at its best. A journey meandering down the coast via Walberswick, Dunwich, Aldeburgh and Orford will reveal a wealth of unusually scenic countryside as well as a variety of near-classic pubs. Snape Maltings, between Aldeburgh and Orford, is the home of the Benjamin Britten/Peter Piers-inspired artistic and musical institution which houses and promotes a wide variety of artistic pursuits; there are excellent teas, too!

Heading south and skirting the seaward side of Ipswich you will cross the massive concrete expanse of the Orwell bridge. On landing, look out for the A137 turning, signposted Manningtree. Turning towards Ipswich and then almost back on yourself one mile later, you should eventually hit the Shotley road (B1456). The road wanders out into nowhere and eventually comes to the village of Chelmondiston, where a signpost to the left reveals the road down to Pin Mill.

There is a body of opinion that states that there is no such thing as a fisherman's pub, it is just a tale exaggerated by anglers! If such an opinion is wrong then Pin Mill's Butt & Oyster is the pub that gives it the lie.

Close to an increasingly popular marina, this rambling old pub reeks of sailing folk. Dating back to the seventeenth century, its interior design is in a classical style. There is a new bar at the end, into which much of the chips-in-a-basket custom has been decanted. The main bar is unquantifiably nautical. The beer straight from the barrel, the deep-hued wooden fittings, the tiled floor and the old fireplace that cries out for a huddle of salty dogs with clay pipes and waterproofs all combine to produce its splendid atmosphere. There is also a side bar for quieter folk.

The view from outside stretches right down the estuary; at low tide over mud flats, at high water over the coal-black sea, with fishing boats bobbing. Maybe it is the last of the authentic maritime inns.

Butt & Oyster
Pin Mill, nr Ipswich, Suffolk
☎ Woolverstone (047384) 224
11-2.30; 5 (7 in winter)-11

Tolly Cobbold Mild, Bitter, Original, Old Strong

Families welcome. Lunchtime & evening food. Garden.

W e now head back towards Ipswich, and on joining the bypass, look out for the A1071 turning to Hadleigh. Although the A45 is quicker, the route through Hintlesham and Hadleigh, up through Kersey and Lindsey to Brent Eleigh will take you through the eastern part of Constable Country. Thatched villages and half-timbered high streets blend into one; gentle hills and winding lanes take you through one of the most beautiful parts of the rural South and detours are both tempting and rewarding.

Sam Potter's Cock, as the pub is universally known, may be old but it is still in full working order. A thatched roadhouse on an all but forgotten highway, it pretends to be nothing in particular. Sam keeps the beer out the back and brings it to the bar in unhurried fashion – at Suffolk pace. He will sit and yarn, even though he may not have met you before and is unlikely to meet you again.

The 'saloon' bar is barely large enough to swing a cat, not that anyone would attempt such exercise. The main bar is in the old style: a single large table for gathering around, and a dartboard to its side for the energetic. If you are in luck you will coincide with the old 'bors'. Skilled linguists have been foiled by such as these with conversation in broadest 'Suffik' about subjects as obscure as the vowel sounds. Pidgin Punjabi is simple compared to this dialect.

Cock
Licensee: Sam Potter
Brent Eleigh, nr Lavenham Suffolk
☎ Lavenham (0787) 247407
11-2.30; 6-11

Greene King IPA

Garden.

The easy way to reach Bury St Edmunds is to take the road to Lavenham, perhaps the most perfectly preserved medieval town in England, then carry on via Cockfield to the main A134 and turn right; but this is forgotten England and a tour is justified.

In the fifteenth century, Lavenham, Hadleigh, Long Melford and Bury St Edmunds were numbered amongst the largest towns in England, but whilst others grew, these shrunk. Though their significance dwindled, much of their architecture remains. The ridiculously outsized churches of both Lavenham and Long Melford bear witness to this. Melford's High Street stretches the best part of one and a half miles, though its population is well below ten thousand. This was the last place where the Riot Act was read, following an attempt at vote-rigging at a general election by local Tories. Nowadays its antique shops almost outnumber its population.

From Melford, a circular tour via Glemsford and Cavendish to Clare, then north to Poslingford, Hawkedon, Hartest and Shimpling will take you through areas almost entirely depopulated, yet only fifty miles as the crow flies from London.

However you get to Bury St Edmunds, the first thing you will realise about this Georgian market town is that a pub in its centre is not strictly a 'country' pub; and I confess that I have bent the rules slightly to include the Nutshell in my list. It is an exceptional pub, however, even without its chief claim to fame, that of being the smallest pub in the world.

You will find the tiny place on a side street off the main market square. Its floor space is barely over a hundred square feet and when more than eight people are drinking there it is full. Yet surprisingly, evening trade is light and you will be unlucky not to find space either to stand or sit. Be warned that on one occasion 101 people and a dog were squeezed in, without any standing on shoulders.

Despite its size, it would be easy for such a place to become ordinary, just another stop on the round Britain sight-seeing trip. The fact that it is a first-rate pub is due to its landlady and an extraordinary collection of *objets d'art*. If you have any examples of 'The Smallest', then all donations are gratefully received. A miniature copy of *The Times*, the smallest dartboard and snooker table, a mini-loo and a Department of the Environment approved miniature dustbin nestle alongside

Nutshell
Licensee: Shirley Pepper
The Traverse, Bury St Edmunds, Suffolk
☎ Bury St Edmunds (0284) 64867
11-2.30; 7-11 (Closed Sunday and Public Holidays; market licence till 5 p.m. Wednesday and Saturday)

Greene King XX, IPA, Abbot

Sandwiches most times.

such items as an elephant's tooth, a three-legged chicken, a disused left leg and a mummified cat and mouse! The international appeal of the place is obvious from the collection of banknotes from across the continents, but despite this most of the customers are local.

The only qualification for admission is a willingness to talk about anything to anyone else who happens to be there; you really do not have the option. If you find that difficult, never fear. Shirley Pepper can give you a potted history of the place in her sleep and loves 'the chat'. It has a market licence to open all day on Wednesday and Saturday, but

A former museum, the Nutshell at Bury St Edmunds boasts a collection of miniature curios
Opposite: The smallest of the small, the Nutshell nestles on a street corner

uses it with caution. To be honest, the place is best avoided on Saturdays before 7 p.m., when the market day crowds spill out on to the pavements like volcanic lava, but of an evening it can be priceless.

The road west from Bury comes first to Newmarket, the racing centre of East Anglia, and the opulence of the paddocks along the town's approach roads should warn the observant about the fate of their stakes. On the other side of town the old Roman road stretches majestically over the flats and on towards Cambridge.

One of the delights of Cambridge is punting along the 'Backs' where the lawns of the great colleges stretch down to the Cam. As at Oxford, the choice of things to see is almost overwhelming, but Christopher Wren's superb library at Trinity College and

The Queen's Head
Licensee: David Short
Newton, nr Cambridge.
☎ Cambridge (0223) 870436

Adnam Bitter, Old (winter brew)

Lunchtime food. Outside drinking area.

The Queen's Head at Newton; King George and the Kaiser drank here before the First World War

the King's College Chapel would be on most shortlists. Explore the streets and the winding, narrow lanes and passages, then take the A10 out of the city towards Royston, turning off not far beyond the motorway to the village of Newton, and its historic pub, the Queen's Head.

The Queen's Head in question belongs to Anne of Cleves, though no one knows why, as she has no links with the area. The pub stands at the meeting of five roads, and once offered accommodation to travellers on the London to Ely coaching route. The building dates back to 1680 and is of unusual design, with an imposing tall chimney, a small, comfortable lounge and a larger bar with an impressive fireplace and scrubbed benches. A short passage from the bar leads into a room, more a swelling off the passage, where darts and other games are played.

The pub was originally a farm, brewing ale as a side-line. As the importance of the road increased, so did that of ale-brewing, encouraging the owner to make his building an inn. Though Anne of Cleves is not thought to have dropped in, King George and the Kaiser enjoyed a drink on the green in the halcyon days before the First World War, and the Shah of Iran and his wife had lunch there twenty years ago. Good pub lunches are served at the Queen's Head seven days a week, and the pub has a warm and timeless quality enriched by the welcome from staff and regulars.

The seventeenth-century Axe & Compasses in the picturesque village of Arkesden

Leaving Newton, take the back road over to Whittlesford and drive south, parallel to the M11, on roads which are not as fast, but infinitely more pleasant. Pause, perhaps, at the great sweep of lawns and the stately home at Audley End, and look at the nearby town of Saffron Walden, with its impressive marketplace and stunning architecture. Head west on the B1039, and quite soon you will reach a turning on the left that takes you to the village of Arkesden.

It is a fine and picturesque Essex village, much photographed, with houses and cottages set back from the road and screened by trees and bushes. The pub, the Axe & Compasses, is a fascinating architectural mix: a tall, thatched building, dating back to 1650, with a smaller weatherboarded section added in the early nineteenth century.

The newer section is now the public bar and houses a pleasing mixture of old and new villagers. The bar is low-ceilinged and dominated by the large serving area that links it with the plush lounge, reached by a short passageway. The lounge is a higgledy-piggledy mixture of standing and seating areas, leading to a separate dining area. The pub and the customers are friendly and welcoming and the solitude of the village is remarkable for an area so close to the M11 motorway.

From Arkesden, head back up to the B1039 through Duddenhoe End and carry on west to Barley. Stop at the Fox & Hounds there, if you feel like a glass of their home-brewed beer and a look at their unusual and famous 'gantry' sign, then turn south on the B1368. In the village of Barkway you will see a right turn that will lead you to the village of Reed and the last classic pub on our long journey round Britain.

The village is just a few minutes from the busy A10 London to Cambridge road, yet has a pleasing calm and tranquillity. Reed dates back to the time of the 'Domesday Book', and the size of the population today is the same as when William the Conqueror ordered his great survey. The Cabinet at Reed is a traditional East Anglian weatherboarded pub with a free-standing pub sign. There is a large garden with plenty of benches and seats for sunny weather.

The pub has had an ale licence since the sixteenth century and was originally a one-bar house. The lounge was added just thirty years ago, and is a pleasant, if characterless addition. The heart of the pub, and of the village, is the remarkable bar, tiny, yet full of corners and hideaways. The only blemish is the

The Axe & Compasses
Licensee: Gerry Roberts
Arkesden, nr Saffron Walden, Essex
☎ Clavering (079 985) 272
10.30-2.30; 6-11

Greene King Abbot; Rayment BBA

Food: lunchtimes & evenings Tuesday to Saturday. Garden.

The Cabinet
Licensees: Andrew & June Johnson
Reed, nr Royston, Hertfordshire
☎ Barkway (076 384) 366
11-2.30; 6-11

Adnam Bitter, Extra (in summer); Hook Norton Bitter; Mauldon Bitter, Special; Guest beers

Lunchtime food. Garden.

modern gas fire that has been stuck, as an afterthought, into the traditional fireplace.

The doorway into the bar is treacherously low, an indication of how much shorter our forebears were. To your right is a small alcove with tables and chairs. A few steps down and you are in the main body of the bar; a roaring fire to one side; the serving area, with the beer stillaged behind the bar, to the other.

Publican Andrew Johnson believes that the unusual name of the pub stems from the time when French Huguenots settled in the area and wanted a meeting-place, a cabinet, in which to hold discussions and, no doubt, partake of the strange English ale.

The Cabinet at Reed, once a meeting-place for French Huguenots, now the meeting-place for the whole village

The marathon journey is now almost at an end; you can be in London in little more than an hour. On your travels round Britain you will have seen wild moorlands and rocky coastlines, wooded valleys and rolling downlands, sleepy hamlets and beautiful villages. You will have been in great coaching inns and tiny village locals, eaten wonderful food and drunk marvellous beer, and you will have got to know more about Britain and the British in the time taken to visit these one hundred classic country pubs than you would in a lifetime of watching the television and reading the newspapers.

The British pub remains the heart of our communities and the focus of our social life. This hundred could have been a thousand or even ten thousand – long may they all continue to delight us with their character, their atmosphere and their warm and friendly welcome.

Page 190: The sunny interior of the Mason's Arms, Strawberry Bank

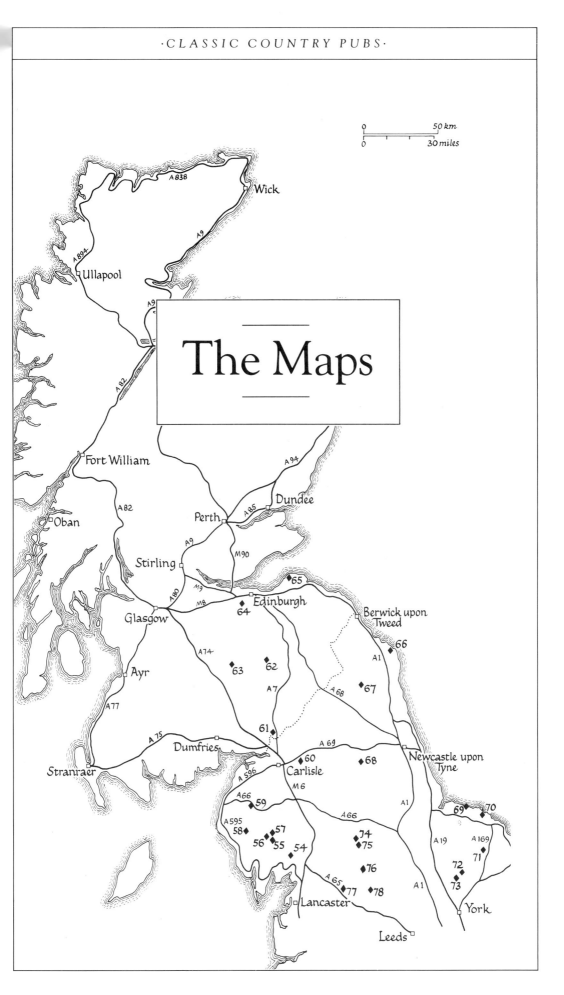

The Maps

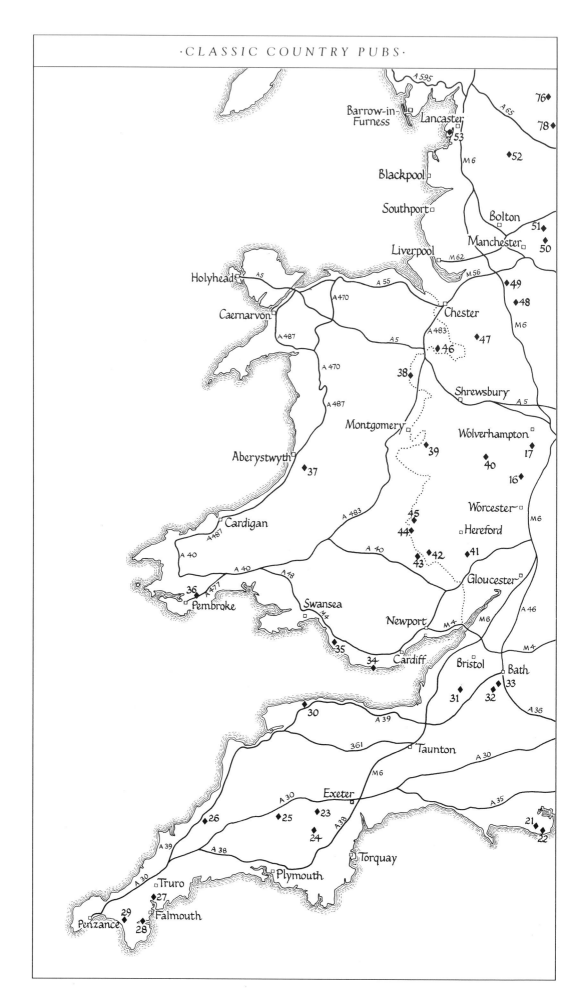

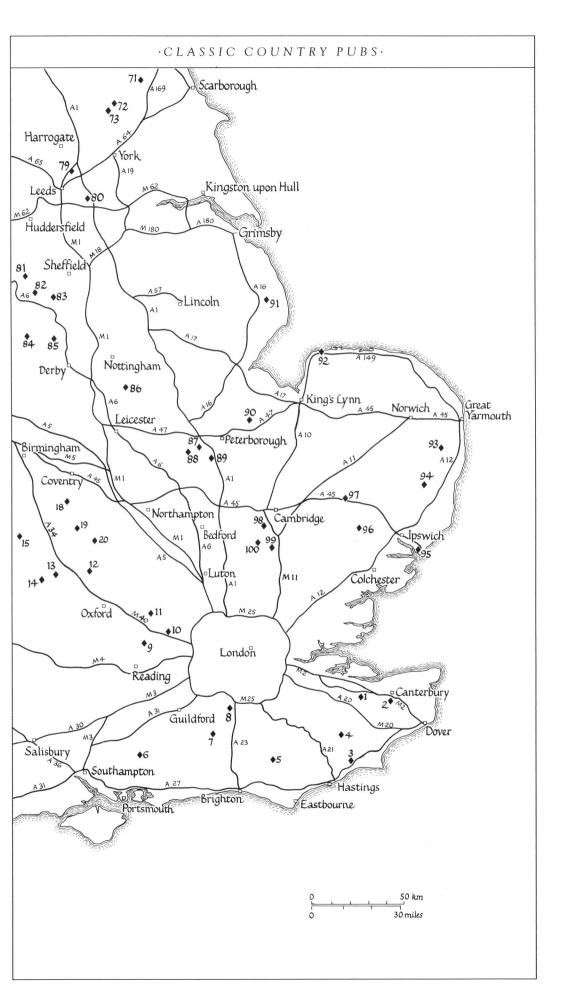

Index of Pubs

Map references are in bold numerals, page references are in italics.

To the Garden of England & the Downs

1 The Carpenters Arms, Eastling, Kent *24*
2 The Duck Inn, Pett Bottom, Kent *25*
3 The Mermaid, Rye, East Sussex *26*
4 The Three Chimneys, nr Biddenden, Kent *29*
5 The Blackboys Inn, Blackboys, East Sussex *31*
6 The White Horse, Priors Dean, Hampshire *33*
7 The Punch Bowl, Oakwood Hill, Surrey *34*
8 The Skimmington Castle, Reigate Heath, Surrey *35*

To Oxford & Shakespeare Country

9 The Crooked Billet, Stoke Row, Oxfordshire *38*
10 The Royal Standard of England, Forty Green, Buckinghamshire *39*
11 The Lions of Bledlow, Bledlow, Buckinghamshire *40*
12 The Falkland Arms, Great Tew, Oxfordshire *42*
13 The Fox Inn, Broadwell, Gloucestershire *43*
14 The Plough, Ford, Gloucestershire *44*
15 The Fleece Inn, Bretforton, Hereford & Worcester *47*
16 The Plough, Shenstone, Hereford & Worcester *48*
17 The Crooked House, Gornal, West Midlands *49*
18 The Case is Altered, Haseley Knob, Warwickshire *50*
19 The Rose & Crown, Ratley, Warwickshire *53*
20 The George & Dragon, Chacombe, Northamptonshire *54*

To the West Country

21 The Fox, Corfe Castle, Dorset *56*
22 The Square & Compass, Worth Matravers, Dorset *57*
23 The Drewe Arms, Drewsteignton, Devon *58*
24 The Rugglestone Inn, Widecombe-in-the-Moor, Devon *60*
25 The Castle Inn, Lydford, Devon *62*
26 The St Kew Inn, St Kew, Cornwall *64*
27 The Pandora Inn, Restronguet Creek, Cornwall *65*
28 The New Inn, Manaccan, Cornwall *66*
29 The Blue Anchor, Helston, Cornwall *68*
30 The Hunters Inn, Parracombe, Devon *70*
31 The Ring o' Bells, Compton Martin, Avon *73*
32 The Tuckers Grave, Faulkland, Somerset *74*
33 The George, Norton St Philip, Somerset *75*

To Wales & the Welsh Borders

34 The Blue Anchor, East Aberthaw, South Glamorgan *78*
35 The Prince of Wales, Kenfig, Mid Glamorgan *80*
36 The Carew Inn, Carew, Dyfed *83*
37 The Halfway Inn, Pisgah, Dyfed *84*
38 The Horseshoe, Llanyblodwel, Clwyd *86*
39 The Three Tuns, Bishops Castle, Shropshire *88*
40 The Fox & Hounds, Stottesdon, Shropshire *89*
41 The Cottage of Content, Carey, Hereford & Worcester *91*
42 The Trout Inn, Dulas, Gwent *92*
43 The Abbey Hotel, Llanthony, Gwent *94*
44 The Blue Boar, Hay-on-Wye, Hereford & Worcester *94*
45 The Rhydspence Inn, Whitney-on-Wye, Hereford & Worcester *97*
46 The Boat Inn, Erbistock, Clwyd *98*

To the Lake District

47 The Dusty Miller, Wrenbury, Cheshire *100*
48 The Swettenham Arms, Swettenham, Cheshire *101*
49 The Bells of Peover, Lower Peover, Cheshire *102*
50 The Horse & Jockey, Delph, Greater Manchester *105*
51 The Ram's Head, Denshaw, Greater Manchester *107*
52 The Inn at Whitewell, Forest of Bowland, Lancashire *108*
53 The Golden Ball, Snatchems, Lancashire *109*
54 The Masons Arms, Strawberry Bank, Cumbria *111*
55 The Drunken Duck, Barngates, Cumbria *112*
56 The Britannia Inn, Elterwater, Cumbria *114*
57 The Old Dungeon Ghyll Hotel, Langdale, Cumbria *116*
58 The Wasdale Head Hotel, Wasdale Head, Cumbria *116*
59 The Pheasant Inn, Bassenthwaite Lake, Cumbria *118*

To the Scottish Borders

60 The Hare & Hounds, Talkin Village, Cumbria *120*
61 The Riverside Inn, Canonbie, Borders *122*
62 The Gordon Arms, Yarrow, Borders *124*
63 The Crook Inn, Tweedsmuir, Borders *125*
64 The Grey Horse, Balerno, Lothian *128*
65 The Castle Inn, Dirleton, Lothian *129*
66 The Olde Ship Inn, Seahouses, Northumberland *130*
67 The Star, Netherton, Northumberland *132*
68 The Lord Crewe Arms, Blanchland, County Durham *133*

To the Yorkshire Moors and Dales

69 The Ship Inn, Saltburn-by-the-Sea, Cleveland *136*
70 The Royal, Runswick Bay, North Yorkshire *137*
71 The Blacksmiths Arms, Lastingham, North Yorkshire *138*
72 The Star, Harome, North Yorkshire *140*
73 The Malt Shovel, Oswaldkirk, North Yorkshire *141*
74 The Tan Hill Inn, Keld, North Yorkshire *143*
75 The Farmers Arms, Muker, North Yorkshire *146*
76 The White Lion, Cray, North Yorkshire *148*
77 The Game Cock, Austwick, North Yorkshire *149*
78 The Fountaine Inn, Linton-in-Craven, North Yorkshire *151*
79 The Bingley Arms, Bardsey, West Yorkshire *152*
80 The Chequers, Ledsham, West Yorkshire *154*

To the Peak District & the Midlands

81 The Old Nags Head, Edale, Derbyshire *156*
82 The Old Bulls Head, Little Hucklow, Derbyshire *157*
83 The Chequers, Froggatt Edge, Derbyshire *160*
84 The Yew Tree, Cauldon, Staffordshire *160*
85 The Barley Mow, Kirk Ireton, Derbyshire *163*
86 The Crown, Old Dalby, Leicestershire *164*
87 The Falcon, Fotheringhay, Northamptonshire *165*
88 The Shuckburgh Arms, Southwick, Northamptonshire *166*
89 The Bell Inn, Stilton, Cambridgeshire *168*

To the Fens, the Broads & Constable Country

90 The Four Horseshoes, Throckenholt, Lincolnshire *172*
91 The Blacksmiths Arms, Skendleby, Lincolnshire *173*
92 The Lifeboat, Thornham, Norfolk *176*
93 The Locks, Geldeston, Norfolk *176*
94 The Kings Head, Laxfield, Suffolk *178*
95 The Butt & Oyster, Pin Mill, Suffolk *180*
96 The Cock, Brent Eleigh, Suffolk *180*
97 The Nutshell, Bury St Edmunds, Suffolk *181*
98 The Queen's Head, Newton, Cambridgeshire *182*
99 The Axe & Compasses, Arkesden, Essex *185*
100 The Cabinet, Reed, Hertfordshire *185*